A LIFE
WELL PLAYED

A LIFE
WELL PLAYED

————— MY STORIES —————

The Commemorative Edition

ARNOLD PALMER

ST. MARTIN'S PRESS ✹ NEW YORK

www.stmartins.com

Endpaper photos courtesy of APE and the Associated Press. Interior photos courtesy of Pete Fontaine.

Designed by Steven Seighman

The Library of Congress has cataloged the hardcover edition as follows:

Names: Palmer, Arnold, 1929–2016 author.
Title: A life well played : stories and wisdom from on and off the golf
    course / Arnold Palmer.
Description: First edition. | New York : St. Martin's Press, [2016]
Identifiers: LCCN 2016013252 | ISBN 9781250085948 (hardcover) |
    ISBN 9781250085955 (ebook)
Subjects: LCSH: Palmer, Arnold, 1929–2016 | Golfers—United
    States—Biography. | Conduct of life.
Classification: LCC GV964.P3 A3 2016 | DDC 796.352092 [B]—dc23
LC record available at https://lccn.loc.gov/2016013252

ISBN 978-1-250-16107-9 (Commemorative Edition)

Our books may be purchased in bulk for promotional, educational, or business use. Please contact your local bookseller or the Macmillan Corporate and Premium Sales Department at 1-800-221-7945, extension 5442, or by email at MacmillanSpecialMarkets@macmillan.com.

First Commemorative Edition: September 2017

10   9   8   7   6   5   4   3   2   1

CONTENTS

———

LIFE   107

FOREWORD

IT WAS JUST A QUICK GESTURE. And although perhaps glimpsed by thousands, it was meant for the eyes of one: Arnold Daniel Palmer.

When Gary Player and I stepped on the first tee of Augusta National Golf Club on a recent crisp, cool Thursday morning, we were missing something, someone. For the first time in fifty-three years, there was no Arnold Palmer at the Masters, and for the first time since the Big Three were asked to become honorary starters, our friend was not able to make his tee time. Left behind was a Green Jacket draped over an empty chair and countless memories. When it was my turn to make a pass at the ceremonial tee shot, I lifted my hat and my eyes to the sky, simply to let my dear friend know he was missed but never forgotten.

I like to believe that Arnold offered back his trademark wink and a thumbs-up.

Due to the nature of tournament golf, I have, in essence, competed against thousands of fine players in my career. But never in my life did I encounter anyone quite like Arnold Palmer. He was a remarkable individual with a champion's swagger and a common touch, and as many of you who follow golf are aware, he was perhaps the most popular player in the history of the game.

He also was my friendly rival—emphasis on the "friend" part.

I remember when I first saw Arnold Palmer hit a golf ball. I was fourteen years old and it was prior to the 1954 Ohio Amateur at Sylvania Country Club in Toledo. I watched Arnie, then the defending champion, hit short irons like lasers in the rain on the otherwise deserted practice range. Four years later, I played with Arnold for the first time, also in my home state of Ohio, in a four-man exhibition at Athens Country Club. Athens native Dow Finsterwald had just won the PGA Championship, and a day was held in his honor. Earlier that year, Arnold had won his first Masters. I won a driving contest, sending a shot over the first green, and I was happy to remind Arnold of that for many years. He was quick and delighted to remind me that he won the day, with a course record of 62 to my 68.

If there was a genesis to our rivalry, it was likely that day. I will never forget the date: September 25, 1958. And the competitiveness between us never ended until—be it ironic, fitting, or something spiritual—that very day exactly fifty-eight years later when Arnold passed away.

But with the passion that came with Arnold's golf and

our competition, I quickly saw the compassion that would always underlie it. Early in 1962, my rookie year on the PGA Tour, Arnold and I were paired together for the first time in the final round of the Phoenix Open. As we walked off the 17th green, he put his arm on my shoulder. I knew I needed birdie at 18 to finish second. So did Arnold, who told me, "Just relax, it's not a hard par five. You're in good shape. Just play smart and you'll finish second." He didn't have to do that, yet there he was, Arnold Palmer, trying to help a young guy while winning a tournament. I did get my birdie to finish joint second. Arnold nipped me by just twelve strokes.

Several months later, at the U.S. Open, I won my first professional tournament and my first major title, and, of course, Arnold was right there to battle me throughout four rounds and an 18-hole playoff. But I was a twenty-two-year-old with blinders on, having no clue that not only was I battling Arnie, but I was doing so in his Pennsylvania backyard at Oakmont Country Club. I was so intent on winning that I was largely unaware of the partisan galleries who did not like this upstart kid trying to take down their giant, the universally popular Arnold Palmer. But again that day Arnold could not have been nicer to me, and again showed his grace by offering to split the gate that historically went to the winner. Arnold was a sportsman to the end, congratulating me with genuine sincerity.

Arnold came along at a time when golf needed him most. When TV first embraced the sport of golf, they had a swashbuckling hero in Arnold as the game's face. He was the everyday man's hero. He embodied the hard-working strength of America. With his shirt often hanging out and a hitch of his pants, Arnold played a game we could all appreciate. He made the recovery shot a form of art. And people adored it.

He appealed to everyone. When he slipped on a Green Jacket, you might say he was comfortable wearing a blue collar or white collar beneath it. He exuded a kind of coolness that was difficult to describe but impossible not to notice. But his charisma came with a softness, a smile, a wink, and, yes, that thumbs-up.

It was hard for anyone to compete with that kind of charm, and I was smart enough to know that. Instead, our rivalry was on the golf course, where we tried our darndest to beat each other. Sometimes we focused so intently on what the other was doing that we lost sight of the big picture, which was winning the golf tournament, and someone else would sneak by us on the leaderboard. Yes, we had our backs up, you might say, in the heat of competition, but we also had each other's back if ever one of us needed the other. And that occurred many times over the course of six decades.

I think Arnold captured the spirit of our friendship and rivalry in one of the sections of this book, and I was tickled to read about our "competition" in the area of autographs. I won't give away the details here, but suffice it to say that the tale is one more example of the never-ending saga of Jack vs. Arnie.

The stories that Arnie shares in his final literary effort are a wonderful compilation that reflect who he was as a person, as a golfer, and as someone who believed in giving back. He was a champion at each turn, and it was an honor not just knowing him and competing against him for nearly sixty years, but also being his friend.

By the way, after Gary and I hit our tee shots on April 6, 2017, to christen the 81st Masters, I slipped on my Green Jacket, and along with it, a button over my left chest—somewhere close to my heart—that read, "I am a member of Arnie's Army." This book represents a final chance for all of us in Arnie's Army to embrace him one more time. So sit back and enjoy the journey.

—Good golfing,
Jack Nicklaus

A LIFE
WELL PLAYED

INTRODUCTION

———

EVERY PART OF MY GAME and every part of my life truly has been the product of the influence of my father, Milfred Jerome "Deacon" Palmer, or Deke as he was known to practically everyone. I begin with this thought because I began my journey through this golfing life with Pap's unswerving guidance as the bedrock of just about everything I tried to do and how I chose to do it. My whole being has been a reflection of him. I wanted to emulate him, I wanted to be as tough as he was, and I wanted to do the things he did in the right way, as he did them.

I was the first of four children to Deke and Doris Palmer, two kindhearted people who knew the value of hard work and who valued integrity, respect, and manners. My father would come to be the most influential person in my life because of the amount of time I spent with him from an early age, and what he taught me was everything that came to be important about how to play golf and how to live my life.

It's no stretch to say that the direction of my life was set when my father, at fifteen, quit school to go to work at American Locomotive in Latrobe but found he didn't like being indoors. When he learned that a golf course was being built a couple of miles from his parents' house in Youngstown, he jumped at the chance to help, and got a job on a three-man construction crew digging ditches. He knew nothing about golf or growing grass or shaping a fairway, but, nevertheless, he was asked to stay on to maintain the course when it was completed. He literally learned on the job to be a greenskeeper, and later the club's golf pro.

I practically grew up at my father's side. When my sister Lois Jean came along two years after me, Pap would take me with him to work so that my mom could keep a handle on my sister and things at home. Therefore, I was around my father all day every day and around golf all day every day. There was really no way my immersion in Pap's environment wasn't going to have a huge influence on me. I was three when Pap put my hands on a golf club, showing me the overlapping grip, and he told me, sternly, "Now don't ever change that." Though I would go off on my own and practice and experiment—occasionally at times when I wasn't supposed to—Pap taught me the proper fundamentals of the stance, alignment, and the basis of the swing. He also put me to work around the golf course and in the pro shop, and I learned a great deal about other aspects of the game.

Most important of all, he taught me to be a sportsman, to

show good sportsmanship, and there were plenty of times he reminded me of this until it was ingrained in my mind. In addition, good golf etiquette was mandatory. You fix your ball marks and divots, you don't walk ahead of your partners, you remain still when a fellow player is hitting a shot, and so forth.

But he didn't just teach me to play golf. He taught me a discipline that things should be done a certain way—as well and as hard as you can.

Pap was a tough, taciturn disciplinarian. I don't want to say that I was afraid of him, but he certainly always had my attention, and if he told me to do something, I got it done as fast as I could. He wasn't one to mince words, make excuses, or abide sloppiness of thoughts or actions. He believed in hard work and being a good person, and there wasn't a lot of room in his mind for slacking off in either regard. He was highly strong-minded, something else he passed on to his son.

What he rarely passed on to me were many compliments. He rode me hard, and as I improved as a golfer I still had to prove to him that I was good. And I always wanted to show him. Trying to tell him so would never do, anyway, because he often said that if you're good at something, you don't have to tell anyone. You show them. That was his way of reminding me to be humble, and I always tried to keep that in mind. He also wanted me to be humble in how I treated others. I think that was the product of his simple upbringing. He was never going to let anyone think they were better than him; conversely, he didn't want his son thinking he was any better than anyone else. You treat people with respect and dignity, regardless of who they are or what they do, and you darn well better have proper manners. He taught me not only how to hold a golf club, but also how to hold a fork and a spoon and a knife. He taught me how to say "please" and "yes sir" and "no sir."

Obviously, these were important lessons. But I didn't learn everything from Pap. Along the way I was so lucky to have amazing people come along at the right time and further shape by life, starting with Winnie Walzer, whom I courted for all of about ninety-six hours before I decided that I wanted her to marry me. Winnie was truly my better half, someone who was supportive of everything I was trying to do and knew me almost as well as I knew myself. She knew my moods, and she would help with my attitude and outlook. A friend to everyone who knew her, Winnie was selfless beyond compare. And she was wise. Her advice and good sense were indispensable, especially after I lost my father in 1976.

Then there was Mark McCormack, who made such a huge impact on my career. Mark was brilliant, and he did amazing things on my behalf. Our partnership made us successful far beyond anything I could ever have imagined. And although I had so many wonderful friends through the years, no one compared to President Dwight Eisenhower. He was like another father to me. Our conversations were always something that gave me great comfort or food for thought. He had the kind of attitude and positive outlook that were an inspiration to me.

And, of course, always my constant companion has been the game of golf, a game of grace and mystique, a pursuit from which I have never stopped learning. There are so many wonderful aspects to being a golfer. It's an endless challenge, one that can't be perfected but sometimes can be done with such transcendent skill that it just lifts the soul. And even the most inexperienced, raw golfer can feel that thrill on occasion because there's just a certain inner satisfaction in going out and hitting a good golf shot. Equally, there is something special about walking around a golf course in the open air, smelling the grass and appreciating the wonders of nature. The people I have met have made my life special. If you're a golfer reading this, think about how many people you've met and made friends with because you played golf. Then take another person who doesn't play golf. I don't care where you are or what sport you're in, it can't compare, in my mind, to golf in bringing people together. Golf is a world in itself. It's an experience that's really worth living.

It's been a wonderful life, I must say, and I say so with all humility and with appreciation for the people who made it so special. I hope the following pages adequately express that sentiment and that they illuminate for you some of those important things I learned along the way.

GOLF

THE GOLF SWING

"HIT IT HARD, BOY, go find it, and hit it hard again."

Those early words from my father formed the very essence of my approach to golf from a very young age. From the beginning I took his advice to heart, and as a young boy I sometimes swung at the ball so hard I nearly toppled over. I remember how a prominent member at Latrobe Country Club once saw me take a cut at the ball and commented to my father that he better do something to fix my swing. My father leveled his gaze at the man and said, simply, "You let me worry about my kid, and you just take care of your own game."

When I began to have some success in junior golf, well-meaning people would watch me slug a golf ball with my homemade corkscrew swing that relied a lot on my upper body strength, and they would offer me well-meaning tips on ways to improve it—as if it needed improving. I just knew it worked for me, and no one was going to convince me otherwise. Pap's basic premise was that once you had the proper grip and understood the fundamental motion behind the swing, the trick was to find the swing that worked best for you and your body type, maximizing your power.

And I wasn't going to let doubters get to me, either. I remember very early in my rookie year hitting balls at Chick Harbert's club in Detroit when I realized that George Fazio and Toney Penna were standing there watching me. Penna was practically a ball-striking legend. Well, I wanted to impress them, so I took some strong cuts with my driver to send balls to the other side of the practice range. I figured they would marvel at my power. After a few swings, I heard Penna ask Fazio if he knew who I was. Fazio replied, "That's Arnold Palmer; he just won the National Amateur."

Then I heard Penna say, "Well, better tell him to get a job. With that swing of his he'll never make it out here." I really burned inside at that remark. And over the first few years of my professional career I heard some similar remarks.

There was no question my swing was unique. I swung my swing, if you don't mind me stealing a line from one of my television commercials. I had one of the biggest turns on tour, with my body rotating far to the right until I had turned my back to the target. My left hip and shoulder swung way around, something neither I nor my father ever really intended. When one fellow professional nudged Pap and asked him if he taught me that turn, he simply responded in his own reserved way, "Now wouldn't that have been a silly thing to do?"

What he meant was that a teaching pro—and my father made himself into an excellent teacher through his own diligence and ability—should never urge his pupils to think a certain way about the turn. I certainly never worried about it because it just occurred naturally in my swing with my hands and arms pulling my body around, something that proved a huge asset. I generated a lot of power with that swing until a hip injury started to slow me down in the late 1960s.

But these kinds of observations continued for some time. Sam Snead once gave me a sort of backhanded compliment. He told reporters that he liked the fluid swings of players like Bert Yancey or Tommy Aaron compared to mine. But, he added, "If they ever had the determination of Arnold Palmer they would do better."

No one was more critical of my game than Ben Hogan.

I'd seen Ben Hogan at various tournaments, but I didn't meet him until the Masters in 1955. To be honest, I was so in awe of the man, and so naturally shy, I felt he was utterly unapproachable. At Augusta someone introduced us, and we shook hands. He was polite enough, but I felt the cool distance others sensed while in his presence. Hogan was still limping from his 1950 car crash but remained the most dangerous player of his age, maybe the best ball-striker who ever lived. I was at first surprised by—and later angered about—the fact that he never, in the years I knew him, called me by my first name. Ten million golf fans have felt completely comfortable calling me "Arnie," but Hogan never called me by name. He only called me "fella," even when I played for him in the Ryder Cup.

Three years after that first meeting, my good friend Dow Finsterwald set up a practice-round game against Hogan and Jackie Burke at Augusta on Tuesday morning. Because I was in a Monday playoff at the Azalea Open in Wilmington, I didn't arrive in Augusta until late that night. Well, more like early Tuesday. I played very poorly, but we took $35 apiece off the two Texans, thanks to Dow. After the match, as I was changing my shoes in the locker room, I heard Hogan talking to Burke, and he wondered aloud, loud enough for me to hear—perhaps even on purpose—how I had ever been invited to play in the Masters. The words I heard were, "Tell me something, Jackie," he said to Burke. "How the hell did Palmer get in the Masters?"

I was a little disappointed that Hogan talked that way. It was a real blow to my ego. And I knew that much of the source of his criticism was my aggressive style of play and my unique swing, which obviously was the antithesis of his game. Hogan was a precise shotmaker with the most repeatable swing in golf.

But even before Hogan poked at me, I had a strong determination to play well at Augusta. My record there up to that point was decent, but there seemed to be this growing belief that I didn't have the game to win there—or in many other places. In the early months of 1958, I had won at St. Petersburg by closing with a 65 to edge Dow and Fred Hawkins, but I had been in contention several other times without winning, including second in Tijuana, seventh in Panama, second in Baton Rouge, and third in New Orleans.

Why would Augusta be any different, particularly with my low ball flight that was such an ill fit for Augusta National? Well, because I believed in myself and in my golf swing. And I had such strong determination. And I knew deep down that I was playing well enough to win. And, of course, I did just that for my first Masters and second major title after my U.S. Amateur victory.

Golf, of course, is more than just how you swing the club. The fact is, I could easily swing a golf club as pretty as the next guy, but it wouldn't have gotten the job done for me. Sure, my swing was herky-jerky as some of the "experts" called it, but it was effective. And I owned my swing, including that high finish with that bit of a windmill action at the top, which I began using in high school to fight off a strong draw (that sometimes was a strong hook). My swing was the exact opposite of Jack Nicklaus's swing. His power came from the waist down with those tree-trunk legs of his. Mine came from my shoulders and arms and hands.

But the reason my golf swing worked so effectively goes back to a few fundamentals, and not just the proper grip. I understood that keeping my head and feet—the anchor points of the swing—as quiet as possible, enabled me to hit the ball solidly all the time. Especially important was keeping my head very still; it's almost impossible to make a bad swing if your grip is good and you keep your head in place. And although I made a big turn, I kept my swing compact, which further helped me to keep the club under control, even when I swung all out.

I can't tell you how important those basics were over the years. And I can't tell you how satisfying it was to keep making people eat their words. Legendary sportswriter Jim Murray once wrote that my swing "looked like a guy beating a carpet." Maybe so, but it was effective in beating the opposition, too.

TAKEOFF

I'VE NEVER MADE IT a secret that the turning point in my golf career and life was my victory in the 1954 U.S. Amateur championship at Country Club of Detroit. The U.S. Amateur was a big deal in that era, which is one reason why I consider myself a winner of eight major championships, instead of the seven that I'm given credit for in my professional career. When you finish first in such a huge tournament with the kind of talent gathered that week in Detroit, I can tell you that winning it felt like winning a major championship.

I was pretty fortunate to be near the top of my game that week. Just seven months removed from my three-year hitch in the Coast Guard, I was coming off what was perhaps my biggest win to date, the All-American at Tam O'Shanter in Chicago, an event that has long been defunct but was a significant tournament in 1954.

I fought my way through the field at the U.S. Amateur

with a series of cliffhangers, including a rally from 2 down with seven to play in my quarterfinal match against Don Cherry. In the semifinals, I needed a birdie on the 39th hole to subdue Ed Meister. In the final against former British Amateur champion Bob Sweeny, I had fallen behind rather quickly as Bob, who at forty-three was nearly twice my age, sank a succession of lengthy birdie putts. I was 3 down after four holes before I knew it. Walking off the fourth green, he put an arm around my shoulder and said to me, "Arnie, you know there's one consolation: You know I can't keep doing this."

Well, he was right, and eventually my advantage off the tee—I routinely outdrove him by 30–40 yards—began to make a difference. Still, I wasn't able to claim my first lead until the 32nd hole of the 36-hole match. (I guess you could say I was charging even in match play.) I went 2 up when I sank a seven-foot birdie putt on the next hole, and although Sweeny birdied the 35th hole from 15 feet, I still felt in control and was able to close out my 2-up victory.

What's that you ask? Didn't I only win 1-up? Why, yes, come to think of it, I did. At least that's what the record book says.

But in actuality the true score was a 2-up victory. Let me explain.

On the par-4 18th hole I smoked a drive right down the middle of the fairway after Bob had hit a weak fade that ended up in the high fescue rough behind two trees. I hit a 4-iron into the green for my next shot while Bob couldn't even reach the green with a 3-iron because he was blocked out by the trees. Soon after Bob conceded the hole and the match.

On the 18th green, USGA executive director Joe Dey said to me, "Arnie, if you don't mind, we'll call this a 1-up victory." Joe had known what had happened. I smiled and replied, "Joe, I don't care what you call this." All I cared about was that he was going to call me the champion.

In his report on the championship the following week in *Sports Illustrated,* the esteemed golf writer Herbert Warren Wind delivered a riveting account of the championship, including the taut final between Bob and me. But his only reference to the final hole was in passing when he wrote: "Though Sweeny fought back to take the 35th with a 15-footer that he had to hole to keep alive and so carried the match right to the home green, in the opinion of both finalists it was the 33rd that was decisive." So what happened on the 36th hole? Wind doesn't say. Talk about anticlimactic.

And so now you know the rest of the story. Whether it was 1-up or 2-up, who really cares. I just know that the "up" part was next to my name. And my career seemed to just keep going up from there. And I was riding a wave of great fortune at that time that carried over to the following week. I'll get to that soon enough.

MISSING IN ACTION

———

I SHOT MY LOWEST 72-hole score in my first PGA Tour victory, the 1955 Canadian Open at Weston Golf and Country Club, where I came in with a 23-under-par 265 total after rounds of 64, 67, 64, and 70 to beat Jackie Burke by four strokes. My score in relation to par set a Canadian Open record that has yet to be broken

It was a victory I almost didn't get to enjoy, but for the fact that I knew well the rules of golf.

Just as I had been in the third round, I was paired in the final round with Tommy Bolt, who was known as a rather ill-tempered sort, but that was only with a golf club in his hands. He built up quite a reputation because he tended to throw a club here and there in frustration, but he was one of the nicest men you could know. In fact, he sort of took me under his wing in my rookie year, and Winnie and I even traveled with him and his wife, Mary Lou.

With just a few holes left to go my lead was comfortable enough over Jack Burke, the third member of our group, that I wasn't too concerned when I hit a tee shot into the woods left of the fairway. As I was milling about assessing my option on my next shot, I felt a tug on my elbow. It was Tommy, and he whispered to me that I should just chip it out into the fairway. I pulled away and continued to look at my options. I heard what he said, but I had to pretend that I didn't, because getting advice from anybody but your caddie is a two-stroke penalty. All I could think at this point was that he was going to cost me the tournament.

So I go walking forward real fast, pretending to look at the line of the shot to the green through the trees. When I got back close to the ball, Tommy is still hovering nearby, and he says again, this time quite a bit louder, "Chip it out safe. Don't do nothing silly." Well, I'm not worried about doing anything silly. I'm worried about Tommy continuing to do something silly, which is trying to "help" me. He had the best of intentions, granted, but I was getting pretty annoyed.

I still pretended not to hear him, and I continued to pretend to look at my options. Tommy now has turned his back, and before he can turn around again I grab an iron and quickly hit the ball through the trees right at the green. I got there, too. Was I crazy? No. But that choice was the only option I had left to me. I certainly couldn't chip out.

Of course, no one was happier for me than Tommy was when I won the tournament. You can be sure I was darn happy. The breakthrough meant a great deal to me beyond the $2,400 first prize. Unfortunately, my elation was short-lived.

I can honestly say that I probably never putted better in my life than I did those four days at Weston. But something troubling happened in the aftermath of the tournament, something that I didn't even realize until I got to the next event, also in Canada, the Labatt Open at Summerlea Golf & Country Club near Montreal. When I got there I looked in my bag, and my Wilson putter was not in it.

I called club officials at Weston, but nobody had seen it, and neither had the man who caddied for me that week. Somebody apparently had walked off with it sometime after I holed a ten-footer for my last putt of the tournament. There was a lot of excitement in the aftermath. Fans were on the green before I could even pick that last putt out of the hole, and I remember shaking a lot of hands and accepting pats on the back as I was engulfed by well-meaning folks.

The newspapers hailed me as the favorite at Summerlea after my big victory (Gene Littler ended up winning), but no one knew that I had lost my putter. I borrowed a putter from Fred Haas to practice with, and a couple of new putters arrived from Wilson before the tournament began. But those new putters just weren't the same. They didn't have the same feel. Plus, that putter that I lost was hot. By that I mean I had a great deal of confidence in it and felt I could hole putts from anywhere. On the sentimental side, I sure hated to lose the putter that gave me my first PGA title. To this day I've never discovered what happened to it, and it would have been nice to be able to have it for posterity's sake.

Painfully, I learned a new rule that week. Don't let your clubs out of your sight.

BIG PICTURE

———

I WENT TO THE BRITISH Open in 1960 for all sorts of reasons, some of them selfish and personal—for the thrill of playing in an Open Championship and the thrill of playing at the Old Course at St. Andrews.

But my motives were many.

Wouldn't it be just wonderful if we had a sport that was a more prominent means of solving problems around the world? What if golf could be something that brought us together? It might even be that sport could be the focus of political situations, and that it could help solve disagreements, that it could replace war and strife on the front pages of newspapers. I know all of that sounds quite fanciful, but that was how I was thinking.

Couldn't we bring disagreements to the sporting field?

That kind of thing, where we have guys trying their guts out in a Ryder Cup or a Presidents Cup or any of the other international events, and why are they doing it? It's for national pride. That's quite a thing. They are competing in sport, and that is honorable, and it's a far sight better than seeing people going at each other on a battlefield somewhere.

That was an ambition of mine in 1960. There was no better place in the world to try and do that than at the Open Championship at St. Andrews. I feel we have succeeded to some degree. Golf is a worldwide sport with a lot of great tournaments and team events, and there is great interest in those events. And now golf is in the Olympics as well, which is very important. Has it solved a lot of world problems? Well, unfortunately, the answer is no, but I won't give up thinking it can get the conversation toward problem solving started.

Now, there were certainly legitimate golf reasons for me to go to St. Andrews. I had planned on going over to Scotland even before I won the Masters that year. Some people thought that after I won the U.S. Open at Cherry Hills that I suddenly decided to head to St. Andrews to try to complete the "modern" Grand Slam. Well, that wasn't even a thing then, although the concept had been percolating in my mind for some time, and having thought about it for some time, I had cause to mention it in my post-championship interviews with the press.

Indeed, once I won the U.S. Open, I knew I was onto something special, and in the aftermath of my victory at Cherry Hills I mentioned to some media members that, "I've got Grand Slam ideas of my own," as I was quoted in some papers. "I'd like to add the British Open and the PGA Championship to those Masters and U.S. Open championships this year."

It's true that my comments became a more earnest topic of conversation between myself and Bob Drum, a writer friend from the *Pittsburgh Press* who had covered much of my golf for a number of years, on the flight from Denver to the United Kingdom, where I first was going to play in the Canada Cup, an international two-man team competition now known as the World Cup, with Sam Snead before heading to St. Andrews. Drum and I further fleshed out the idea of a Grand Slam that would include the Masters, the two Opens, and the PGA, and when we got to Ireland for the Canada Cup, Drum talked up the concept of such a new achievement in golf to some of the international press members. It sounded like a fine idea to me, especially since I was the one who had a chance to do it, but the whole thing really just evolved from ideas that I had been formulating for some time.

Over the years people have asked me frequently why I went to Scotland, and my answer is that I was truly motivated to be a great player, and I didn't feel like you could be a great player if you couldn't win internationally, something Pap often mentioned. So I had to go to the British Open, and in 1960 I was finally in a financial position to do so. It was not an inexpensive proposition to go there, but now I had the wherewithal to include it in my schedule.

At that time I had a singular focus. The goal was just to win it once; it wasn't a question of winning multiple British Opens or some newfangled Grand Slam. But I had to win it for history's sake. Unfortunately, I didn't win it on that first trip to St. Andrews. I lost by a shot to Australia's Kel Nagle (who passed away in 2015 at age ninety-four), but even losing was a kick; it was something that pleased me very much, the whole experience, and it drove me to keep going. And, of course, I did win the British Open in 1961 and 1962, and I proved a lot to myself—and others—about the quality of my golf game.

But, again, it wasn't all about me. Bottom line, I had great hope for the sport of golf and for the world at large when I went to St. Andrews. And when I returned to St. Andrews just last year for the 144th Open Championship, I felt that renewed sense of hope because of the way the game is being conducted and how much it is embraced around the world. Golf has brought people together and generated a common interest and a bond that so many of us are able to share. That's a great feeling, and it pleases me greatly to know I played a small part in that.

ACES

I'VE MADE 20 ACES in my lifetime, which doesn't sound like very many when you consider I've played golf since I was four years old, but the odds of making a hole-in-one are around 2,500-to-1 for a professional (and 25,000-to-1 for an amateur).

My last ace occurred not long ago, in 2011. I remember it clearly. I was playing a friendly round on the Charger Course at Bay Hill with friends Will Carey, Bill Damron (father of tour player Robert Damron), Dick Ferris, and Bruce Walters on a sunny and breezy afternoon in early November. At the 163-yard par-3 seventh hole, I pulled out a 5-iron—a club that has been very good to me through the years when it comes to aces—and played a shot into a crosswind coming from the left. The ball landed ten feet short and rolled right into the hole. I was pretty excited about it until I got the bill later in the club bar. I'm joking, of course. I was only too happy to splurge a little that evening, hosting a dinner party for some two dozen friends. The wine and the good-natured barbs were flowing that night.

Among my four playing partners and me we figured out that we had made a combined 50 aces. So much for those supposed odds.

It had been eight years since my last previous hole-in-one, which also came at Bay Hill. Another interesting thing about the ace in 2011 was that I was using new Callaway irons for the first time that day. Needless to say, they felt pretty good. I finished with a 79, which allowed me to beat my age by three strokes.

It doesn't matter how long you play the game, it never gets old when you make a perfect shot like that. I was in high school when I made my first hole-in-one, at the short par-3 second hole at Latrobe Country Club. I hit a wedge from 134 yards. My second hole-in-one was at the same hole, also with a wedge.

My first ace as a professional came on the 16th hole at Desert Inn Country Club in the first round of the 1959 Tournament of Champions when I holed a 6-iron. I shot a 2-under 70 that day, but I wasn't very excited about it at the time. The tournament was being played in late April, only a few weeks after I had come up short in defense of my first Masters title, and the setback was still on my mind. When asked about the ace after the round, I told the press, "I'd trade that hole-in-one for a couple of putts I missed in the Masters." I had blown a three-foot par putt at the 17th and a four-footer for birdie at the 18th at Augusta National to finish two strokes behind Art Wall Jr., and those misses sure stuck in my craw.

Easily the most exciting ace of my career came on Wednesday, September 3, 1986, on the third hole at TPC Avenel in Potomac, Maryland. And it didn't come in an official tournament round, nor did it lead to a victory. No, it was during the pro-am for the Chrysler Cup, a tournament on the Senior PGA Tour, but, nevertheless, it was easily among the best shots I've ever made in my career, nailing a 5-iron from 182 yards that looked good all the way and rolled right in the cup.

It looked awfully similar to the shot I had hit the day before on the same hole using the same club from the same distance. That's right, during Tuesday's pro-am round I aced the hole with my 5-iron, which made a bit of news. The next day I got on the tee and there was a larger crowd waiting for me, as well as a television news crew from a local NBC affiliate. I heard one of the spectators say, "Hey, Arnie, I came all this way to see you make another one." I just smiled at him. It never entered my mind about knocking the ball in the hole. But I did it, with cameras rolling, no less. I found out a bit later that I was the first American professional golfer to ace the same hole on consecutive days. According to *Golf Digest,* at the time only five Americans, all amateurs, had ever done that. I've had some things happen to me, but never anything close to that. I'd never heard of anyone doing that before. *Newsweek* and *Time* came to the event later in the week to further cover the occasion, which was flattering.

I got a kick out of Chi Chi Rodriguez's comment afterward when he said, "I thought Arnie walked on water before this. Now I know he does. You could give Clark Kent ten balls and he couldn't do that."

To commemorate the occasion, I have the two golf balls (Maxfli DDH III) from those aces hanging on the wall in my office in Latrobe. Former PGA Tour commissioner Deane Beman had them mounted for me. I cherish that simple plaque that reminds me of two of my fondest days in golf.

AUGUSTA

———

I FIRST VISITED AUGUSTA, GEORGIA, and Augusta National Golf Club while I was still attending Wake Forest College. I remember peering through the fence and wondering—and wishing and hoping and dreaming—if I would ever get the chance to play in the Masters. And, of course, after winning the 1954 U.S. Amateur, my wishes came true when I competed in the 1955 tournament. I won $695.83 for finishing tied for 10th, not a bad debut. I remember my first trip down Magnolia Lane: I thought I'd died and gone to heaven. It was perfect. I don't think I'd ever been more in awe.

I had been playing some pretty rough tournaments on some pretty rough golf courses that winter. But when I went out for my first Masters practice round . . . it's a memory still very fresh in my mind, because it was wonderful. Every bit of it. So well manicured and beautiful. I felt a powerful thrill and unexpected kinship with the place; I think because it was purely devoted to golf, and so was I.

While the Masters is first-class all the way, Winnie and I didn't exactly arrive in town in a similar fashion. The tour rookie and his young wife had traveled the first half of that year living in a trailer that we pulled behind our car, and when we arrived in Augusta, we parked it by the railroad tracks on the other side of Daniel Field.

The golf course, though beautiful, was very difficult and it didn't particularly suit my game with its low, boring shots. I adjusted to Augusta National in time by learning to hit the ball a little bit higher and placing the ball in the right parts of the fairways to offer me the best angles to go into the greens.

I always felt something powerful in Augusta. Something magical. I suppose just about every player who has the privilege of playing in the Masters feels it, too. But the key is, can you harness that feeling? I didn't that first time around, although I had an outside chance of winning when I shot a third-round 72 and followed with a closing 69 after a pair of 76s. My hopes were dashed on the 10th hole that final day when I made a double-bogey. You could say my first Masters ended on the back nine on Sunday.

Augusta is probably the ultimate in terms of presentation of a golf tournament and a golf course, its design and condition. It has been an inspiration in how I try to conduct my golf tournament at Bay Hill. If you are going to emulate a standard, I don't think you can do better than the Masters. That's why I played in fifty of them. And each year I had the same feeling as I drove down Magnolia Lane: "This must be heaven." I also feel a renewed sense of gratitude.

The year after winning my fourth and final Masters as well as my last major title, Clifford Roberts, the chairman of Augusta National and cofounder with the incomparable Bobby Jones, asked me if I had any suggestions about how the golf course could be improved. Now I had just won a fourth Green Jacket, and had done so convincingly by six shots over Dave Marr and defending champion Jack Nicklaus. That win by that wide margin meant a great deal to me, because it meant I finally had a chance to stroll up to the 18th green without a great deal of pressure or concern. I could enjoy the moment.

Given the proceedings of that previous April, I wasn't about to suggest he change one thing. And that's exactly what I told him. But it wasn't out of any sense of self-interest. I just didn't see how the wonderful golf course created by Bobby Jones and Dr. Alister Mackenzie could be made better. I believed it wouldn't have been right to tamper with it. Of course, changes have had to be made over time, and the recent moves to lengthen the layout to 7,445 yards I fully support because of the advancements in equipment that would have made the course obsolete had it not been upgraded.

I have called the changes at Augusta a "quiet evolution, but the overall effect is one of gracious permanence."

I played in my final Masters in 2004. I was invited to become the ceremonial starter in 2007, and it's a role that I regard as special as anything I have done in golf. In 2015

I almost didn't make it to the tee. I had taken a tumble the previous December in my home at Bay Hill and had dislocated my right shoulder. My recovery was going so slowly that I had to forgo playing in the Par-3 Tournament. But on Thursday morning, despite not hitting many balls in the previous four months, I made it to the appointed tee time. I had a cortisone shot a few days before just to make sure I was able to take a decent cut at the ball. That's how much I love the Masters Tournament.

The only thing that matched winning the Masters four times was being invited to join as a member, the first Masters winner extended such a courtesy. I accepted, of course, after thinking it over very carefully for five or six seconds. That was a special day. So was Tuesday, April 4, 1995, when the club dedicated a bronze plaque in my honor to commemorate my four victories, joining Byron Nelson, Ben Hogan, and Gene Sarazen as players given such a wonderful honor. It now rests on a drinking foundation behind the 16th tee. Jack Nicklaus has since joined that club, and rightly so with his record six Green Jackets.

Two years later, in 1997, the city of Augusta inducted me into the Georgia Golf Hall of Fame at a ceremony in downtown Augusta. They commissioned a life-sized bronze statue, and I was given a key to the city.

All of these wonderful things that have come my way since my first Masters, to me, are quite staggering. The honor has always been mine simply to be a part of Augusta and to play in the Masters and to be a part of their history. It's been an honor to be a member of the club. It's been an honor to have won the Masters four times. Whatever contributions folks think I have made to the club and the tournament pale in comparison to what I have gotten out of it.

In the balance it's been nothing short of magical. It's been one of the true pillars in my life and career. It's been a lifetime all its own.

MY VERY BEST GOLF

———

Two of my most favorite personal golf memories occurred not in any official tournament but rather in casual rounds at places that are near and dear to my heart. One was at my course at Bay Hill Club & Lodge and the other came at my boyhood layout, Latrobe Country Club, which I now also own.

The first, which happened quite a few years ago, occurred on the par-3 17th hole on the Championship Course at Bay Hill. I stepped up to the tee, and the hole that day was playing nearly the full length of its 221 yards. I decided that I wanted to hit a 2-iron, but my caddie that day, Tomcat, insisted on a 3-iron. Against my better judgment, I went with the 3-iron, and watched it fly beautifully right at the pin—and into the water short of the green.

"Give me the 2-iron," I ordered as I dropped another ball

from the same place. My partners broke up laughing, but as I stepped up to the ball again, I barked, "Laugh all you want. I'll still make par the hard way." This one was struck just as well, but, of course, it flew a little farther, landing on the green, skipping once, and going right into the hole for a par. The hard way.

I handed the club back to the caddie and gave him an "I told you so" look. But I said nothing. Tomcat, sensing that he needed to defend himself, responded to my withering glare by saying, "No sir, Mr. Palmer, I still say it's a 3-iron. You hit it fat." I could only laugh and continue walking.

Meanwhile, on September 12, 1969, a day I will never forget, I chose just about all the right clubs, made nearly all the right swings, and made every putt I looked at—or so it seemed—when I shot a career-low 60 at Latrobe Country Club. I did this despite making two bogeys. (Pap had to get in a little dig at that a few days later, growling, "What were you doing making two bogeys on a day like that?" He did have a point.)

I knew from the moment I teed off that I could be in for a special day. Some days you just know you're going to hit the ball well, and this was one of those days. And, sure enough, I went out and birdied the first three holes, including a real steal at the third, which was then a par-4 of 442 yards, a long hole at the time. (It's now a par-5.)

Another birdie at the short par-4 fifth was canceled by a bogey at the par-5 sixth hole when I flubbed a chip after being just left of the green in two and then didn't get up and down for par after a poor second chip shot. Fortunately, I was still, as they say, playing one shot at a time and not getting ahead of myself.

I rebounded nicely from that disappointment with a birdie at No. 7 and an eagle at the par-5 eighth (which is now a par-4) and went out in 30 after a par at nine. My second bogey came at the par-3 10th, after three putts, but again I brushed aside the error with birdies at 11 and 12 followed by a good par at the 185-yard par-3 13th.

Now I had arrived at the make-or-break juncture of the round with back-to-back par-5s at 14 and 15, a unique design feature at Latrobe. The first is a dogleg right and the second an uphill dogleg left. I drove the ball splendidly on each hole to set up pair of eagles. Boy, was I pumped. When I birdied the short par-4 16th, I had my sixth consecutive "3" and needed just one more birdie to shoot 59, which in the sport of golf is truly a magical number. At the time, no one on the PGA Tour or the LPGA Tour had carded a 59 in a sanctioned round of golf. Al Geiberger was the first to do it in the second round of the 1977 Danny Thomas Memphis Classic at the Colonial Country Club in Cordova, Tennessee, making one eagle, six pars, and eleven birdies—and no bogeys!

I gave myself reasonable birdie chances at each of the last two holes, both par-4s, but neither putt went in. I had to settle for two tap-in pars and a 60. Not a bad day. Those are truly the rounds a player relishes, when he wonders how he could ever play a bad round of golf again. But, of course, the game just isn't that way. Just when you think you have it figured out, the next time it gets you back.

But I'll say this much: no one has yet to beat that score at Latrobe. Holding the record at my home course remains one of the great accomplishments of my golfing life. I sincerely feel that way about it.

MY BEST TIP

———

THIS IS ONE OF the best scoring tips I can offer. How do I know? Because Jack Nicklaus still abides by the advice.

Early in Jack's rookie season I had observed him practicing little chip shots from the fringe of the practice putting green. Some of the shots were very good but most were . . . not. After observing this for a while, I offered Jack my opinion on this type of short-game situation. Being more than ten years older, I did have a bit more experience, and I merely told him that I had found over the years that my worst putt from the fringe is at least as good as my best chip. Jack wrote in his autobiography that he still uses that tip.

Did he ever pay me back in kind? Well, over the years we have traded a lot of ideas about golf as well as many other things. But he did help me with my game once—about three decades after I helped him.

This was in the early 1990s, and I was getting a lesson

from my old college buddy from Wake Forest, Jim Flick, at the Tradition in Arizona. Flick also was a friend of Jack's, and together they had opened a chain of golf instruction schools. At the time, I was having more trouble than usual with my nemesis—getting enough trajectory on my shots. I had hit the ball with a low, boring trajectory my whole life. As Jim and I were talking, Jack walked over, watched me hit a few shots, and then made some helpful comments.

To be honest, I've never sought much help from Jack—or anyone else for that matter. That goes back to what my father said about not listening to what other players tell you because they might not have your best interests at heart. But in that case, I figured Jack was worth listening to. After all, who in history has been better at hitting the ball up in the air than Jack Nicklaus?

The tip didn't work for me, but that didn't mean I didn't appreciate his offer to help. I most certainly did, and Jack and I often discussed other aspects of the game that probably helped each of us. But everyone has to decide for himself if a piece of advice is worth using. The first order of business is to know your game well enough to be able to make the right decision.

DRIVING

———

THERE'S NOTHING IN GOLF more spectacular and satisfying to the soul and the senses than a perfectly long and straight drive, a drive that takes off like a jet, bores a straight line up toward the clouds, and then finally drops in a long and graceful arc, finding its way unerringly to a spot in the fairway way off in the distance.

A long drive is good for the ego. It also is good for the nerves. It sets you up and puts you in a frame of mind to play the rest of your shots well, and it gives you an opportunity to score, to make a birdie or a stress-free par instead of having to grind it out.

I've said previously, what other people may find in poetry or in art museums I find in the flight of a good drive—that white ball getting smaller and smaller as it flies off into a blue sky. Such a thing is truly inspirational, at least to me. And I have always felt that way, even as a kid.

And it's a true weapon, not only in stroke play but also in match play, to be able to drive the ball well, so well that it has your opponents thinking to themselves.

Earlier in my career I was able to take control of some tournaments with a strong driving game, and certainly I couldn't have pulled off any of my charges without it. The best example, of course, was my final round rally in the 1960 U.S. Open at Cherry Hills.

But here's a little news for you: I didn't really master the driver—if anyone can ever master anything about this game—until I was about thirty-two years old. I must have played at least 3,000 rounds of golf by then over twenty-eight years before I truly had a reliable driving game. That didn't mean I could rely on my driver all the time, but I could rely on it most of the time.

What changed? Well, I broke Pap's golden rule, if you will. I changed my grip—if ever so slightly. And then I made another small change. I did this over the span of thirteen years, and it led to one of the best seasons of my career.

The first adjustment came in the summer of 1949 when I weakened my left hand on the grip of the club. What that means is that I rotated my hand on the club slightly to the left and more underneath the grip. One night during the North and South Amateur that year I was playing gin rummy with my good friend Bud Worsham and one of his brothers, Herman. A third brother, Lew Worsham, who won the 1947 U.S. Open, had been watching me earlier that day, and he noticed that my grip was pretty strong—or more on top of the grip—which contributed to the hard draw that

I normally played—and occasionally to a maddening duck hook. He had made an observation about my grip to Herman, who relayed it to me.

I gave this some thought and eventually came to the conclusion that Lew was right, and that a weaker grip would prevent the club head from coming into the ball from a closed position, and I began a painful experiment. That entire summer was a nightmare as my average scores hovered into the 80s. The temptation to go back to my old grip was almost overwhelming as I was feeling so inept and my game was in total crisis. Yet I stuck to my guns. There I was, an eighteen-year-old kid trying to figure out some largely untried theory. I just felt what I was doing was going to make me a better player.

Finally there was a breakthrough in the fall, at Oakmont Country Club in the Western Pennsylvania Amateur. Oakmont is an incredibly difficult course, one where driving the ball well is crucial. Suddenly, my driving began to come around, and I was able to keep the ball in play without losing any distance and without the fear of hitting some ugly hook. In the final, I defeated five-time champion Jack Benson 10–8 for the greatest victory of my career up to that point.

Fast-forward to early 1962, and I am again beginning to think about my driving. As well as I had been playing— winning two Masters, a U.S. Open, and a British Open—I felt like I could do better. Throughout my career I had been teeing up the ball rather low and near the middle of my stance. I made contact with the ball while the club was still descending. But now I started thinking that I needed to move the ball a bit more forward in my stance and tee it up slightly higher. I figured that would give the club head a split second more time to travel down a straight line. That should provide a bit more accuracy, not to mention put the ball higher in the air, adding some distance.

After working on this new fundamental and struggling in the first four events of the 1962 season, I began to see the change bear fruit. I won the Palm Springs Classic (forerunner of the Bob Hope Classic) thanks to five birdies in a row in the final round. Then I went to the Phoenix Open at Phoenix Country Club, a narrow tree-lined course that I had always dreaded. But I arrived there with a lot of confidence, and, sure enough, I drove the ball beautifully and won the tournament by twelve strokes.

I won eight times that year, including my third Masters and second straight British Open title, and if not for 11 three-putts offsetting another beautiful driving and ball-striking week at the U.S. Open at Oakmont I might not have found myself in a playoff with Jack Nicklaus, who beat me by three over the extra 18 holes.

My only regret about it all was waiting so long to make the changes.

CHECK PLEASE

——————

BECAUSE OF THE PGA RULES in place when I turned professional, I wasn't allowed to keep any prize money, regardless of where I finished in a tournament, for a six-month period of apprenticeship. The exception to this rule was the Masters Tournament, which wasn't run by the tour—and still isn't. I earned $695.83 when I tied for 10th place at Augusta National Golf Club, which, believe me, was not insignificant when I wasn't earning any other prize money.

I collected my first official paycheck on May 28, 1955, when I tied for 25th place at the Fort Wayne Invitational at Coyote Creek Golf Club with rounds of 69-72-72-74-287. The tour handed me a check for $145, and I was off and running to season earnings of $7,958, which ranked 32nd on the money list. Pretty good for half a year's credit, helped immensely by the $2,400 I collected for my first official victory in the Canadian Open that August. Overall, I entered thirty-one official events my first season to average $265 per start. My average finish was 22nd. What really got me through the year was a cool piece of change I picked up after being invited to play in the Greenbrier Open, a pro-am tournament that began in 1948 and was hosted by Sam Snead in White Sulphur Springs, West Virginia. (It later was named the Sam Snead Festival.)

Sam invited Winnie and me personally after we had hit it off at the Masters the month before. Held in late spring, the Festival was not an official tour event, but many tour players competed in it, even though it was opposite an official tournament; that year, played May 12–15, it coincided with the Hot Springs Open, in Arkansas. Ben Hogan wasn't playing much anymore, but he was among the fifty players invited to White Sulphur Springs. The field also featured Snead, Jackie Burke, Ed Oliver, Mike Souchak, Henry Picard, Dow Finsterwald, Peter Thomson, and eventual winner Dutch Harrison. Bob Hope was among the regular amateurs who showed up each year.

I was paired the first two days in the team event with a gentleman named Spencer Olin, who was the chairman of a large chemical firm. Spencer bought our team in the Calcutta, and he proceeded to back up his bet by playing splendidly the first day. Meanwhile, I shot a 69, and we were leading the field. Spencer wasn't nearly as brilliant the next day. In fact, he really struggled and carded a 94. But I managed to hold up my end of the deal with another 69, enabling us to tie for first in the team competition.

I scored even better in the final two rounds, with a 66

and 68, for a 272 total, three behind Harrison in a tie for seventh place in the bunched field. I won $280 of the $10,000 purse. That was nice, but nicer was the parting gift from Spencer, who gave me half of his winnings from the Calcutta. Combined with my individual showing, I left West Virginia with close to $10,000. It sure made up for my tour apprenticeship, in which I had to pass on more than $1,100 in prize money. Spencer, one of the great guys of all time, also was gracious enough to fly Winnie and me to our next stop in his private plane, and I remember thinking as I leaned back in the seat inside that DC-3 that this was the way to travel to golf tournaments.

When we got back to Latrobe, Winnie and I decided to buy a car, and we went to Forsha Motors and bought a brand-new 1955 Chrysler New Yorker with some of our Greenbrier earnings. It was the first new car I ever owned. It was tan with a beige interior. Man, it was a sweet car. The next tournament on the schedule was the U.S. Open at Olympic Club in San Francisco. I got that car going over 120 miles per hour while crossing the Great Salt Lake, which didn't make Winnie too happy. But later that evening I was able to make it up to her. We pulled into Elko, Nevada, and we got a room at an inexpensive casino motel. We went out for dinner—a hamburger and a beer—but before turning in I dropped the change from our grand meal on the roulette table. I put it all on double zero, and it hit. We collected 35 silver dollars.

Boy, were we on a roll.

FOCUS

———

In some ways I always admired the way Jack Nicklaus went about playing golf and the amount of intense concentration he used in the heat of a championship. He could just shut everything outside off and go play. He could be superfocused.

I'm not sure I ever wanted to do that. And I don't think you can just show up one week and do that. You can't just say, "Oh, this is the U.S. Open, I'm going to do it now. I'm going to put the blinders on and just get lost in myself." That wasn't me, and I think my golf would have suffered if I tried to play golf that way.

I know people have wondered if I might have won more if I had spent less time concerning myself with the other side of the ropes and employed a version of tunnel vision. Perhaps. Who knows? Maybe if I had gone to hit balls after every round instead of mingling with sponsors and fans and the media, and maybe if I hadn't responded so much to the galleries I might have won a few more titles. It's possible.

But would I have enjoyed it as much? Heck no! If golf itself had been all that mattered, I can't imagine I would have had a better time, even if I had more trophies. Sure, I would love to have won the four U.S. Opens I almost won, or the two or three PGAs I barely lost. But if I had it to do over again, would I take a different approach? I wouldn't. Let's say I could start over. I could have five U.S. Opens and two PGA Championships and six Masters and a couple more British Opens, but not as many friends? Well, that doesn't sound very good to me. Keep the trophies.

The fact is, I knew how to focus on the task at hand when I needed to. I knew how to be myself as I went through my round, but I also knew how to concentrate and be ready to hit the shot when it was my turn to play. I didn't have to shut myself off from the world for hours at a time to do that.

I definitely think I could have won more major titles, not because of the way I handled things but because of the way I lost the ability to handle things. I probably hit the ball better from 1965 to 1974 than I did when I was winning my major championships. I had greater control of the ball and drove it better. In short, I was very happy with my ball striking, and I still won a number of tournaments.

But I didn't win another major after the 1964 Masters, and I had plenty of chances to do that, including several U.S. Opens. The difference was that I lost my edge mentally. I just wasn't as sharp in my thinking and concentration. I can attribute that partly to a certain amount of satisfaction that I was feeling. My win at Cherry Hills was a career-defining moment for me. And that win took away a bit of my edge. Not much, mind you, but just a tiny bit. My fourth Masters title in '64 gave me more Green Jackets than anyone else in history at the time. But more significantly, I won with a comfortable lead. In my previous three wins, I had to fight down to the wire with all the pressure in the world on my shoulders. I didn't get to enjoy the moment. In 1964, ahead by six strokes, I made the walk up the hill to the 18th green knowing that I was going to win. It was wonderful.

I truly believe I might have won more if not for those experiences, winning those two tournaments in such meaningful fashion. That's not to say I'd give them back. But I'm admitting here that they had an adverse effect on how I approached the rest of my career. I still wanted to win badly, yet I sensed a diminished fire inside me.

It might have only cost me a shot or two over 72 holes, but two shots lost are all it takes to go from winning to a second-place finish. And I had 61 of those.

Yes, I was runner-up almost as many times as I was the winner, and when I've been asked about it, I don't find it at all a moral victory to have come so close so often. It isn't failure, either. It's just not getting the job done when winning was all I ever cared about. And I can trace it all to the mental side of the game.

This should tell you how important that six inches between your ears really is. If I had been as sharp mentally as I was in the early part of my career, and you combined that with the sharpness of my ball striking a bit later, I think

I would have won a lot more. I wish I could go back and change that.

But as for how I went about my job—connecting with the fans, laughing, having fun on the golf course, treating the sponsors and the press and tournament staff like friends or extended family—that part I wouldn't change one iota.

TOOLS

———

I ALWAYS FELT LIKE if I could build the perfect golf club, then I should be able to hit the perfect shot and play the perfect game. That's unrealistic, but it never kept me from trying to achieve it. If someone was going to build one, I wanted it to be me.

I got engaged in club repair and club building at a very young age under the tutelage of the golf pro—my father, who taught me every detail about how to work in the shop. I quickly found I had an ability to work with clubs, and at Latrobe Country Club, repairing clubs for members became one of my regular tasks. And I did a lot of experimenting to learn what worked and what didn't. I'd put them together and take them apart. Most people thought that I was a lot better at taking them apart. I will admit that I was never much of a handyman around the house, but I knew what to do with golf clubs. As my good friend Charlie Mechem once said about me, "Everyone has something that mesmerizes them. For Arnold, it's been golf equipment. It's at the center of his being." It would be hard for me to disagree.

When my interest in clubs grew, so did my tinkering. I never had new golf clubs until I was old enough to buy them. So the ones I did have I tinkered with often, and I learned about the playing characteristics of clubs and how to change them through my own trial and error. In high school I was given a set of clubs by a doctor in Latrobe named Homer Mather, who was a member of the club and a good friend of the family. I used them throughout high school, and I can't tell you how many times I bent, sanded, taped, and re-gripped them. And when I turned professional, I did the same thing with my first sets of Wilson clubs. I never used a stock club; they just didn't feel right.

Mark McCormack once said that if a wizard gave me a divining rod that would point to gold in the ground I would take it home and start fiddling with it so it would point to diamonds, too.

In my heyday I traveled with a vise and a hammer in my car and made repairs anywhere I could find a place to work. An uncle who was a steelworker made a tool for me out of stainless steel that I used to bend the hosel of his irons, making what is known as offset, a condition in which the neck of the iron is in front of the face of the club. To steady my nerves before a big round, particularly the final round of a major championship, I would re-grip all of my clubs. And I always brought along an extra set on tour so I had something to work on in my spare time, because that perfect club sometimes just couldn't wait.

I've mentioned that Ben Hogan and I didn't exactly have a warm and fuzzy relationship, but after I won a couple of Masters and the U.S. Open we at least were cordial to the point that he let me borrow a driver from him. It was an excellent driver, but it wasn't Arnold Palmer's driver until I refinished the club head, put more loft on the face, and gave it more of a gooseneck look. I also built up the grip and shortened the shaft a bit. I won a lot of tournaments with that driver. Some time later when Ben saw the club, he took it out of my bag, waggled it, and said, "What have you done to my club? You've ruined a good driver."

Well, beauty is in the eye of the beholder. Or in the eye of the guy with the hammer, vise, and file. I had plenty of ideas for improving clubs, but not all of them worked out. But I did have some commercial successes when I had my own equipment company, the Arnold Palmer Golf Company. One was the Patented Hosel Design iron. Known as the PHD, it was created with the help of Clay Long, an independent designer who also made some clubs for Jack Nicklaus. The iron had a tab of metal on the hosel that allowed weight to be removed from around the face and relocated past the heel of the club. It was basically an oversized game-improvement iron, one of the first of its kind. There was a lot more than just playing better golf that lured me to the workshop. I found refuge and renewal when I went off by myself to tinker with my clubs. One is that I was working with my hands trying to refine something to make it better, which took precision and concentration. The second benefit is that my mind was thrown deeply in the flavor of golf—not necessarily the competitive trials of a particular day or round, but simply golf in deep, enduring, visceral terms that rose out of my childhood. I was going back to my roots, and that is something soothing and inspiring.

Over the years, as I've changed equipment, manufactured my own with the Arnold Palmer Golf Company (which I eventually sold), and received plenty of others from all corners of the globe, I've managed to acquire quite a collection. By a conservative estimate, I must have more than 10,000 clubs and 2,000 putters stored away in buildings and workshops in Latrobe and Orlando. In my workshop in Latrobe, just a few steps from my office, I have hundreds of clubs in bags and in bins, some of which are in various states of transformation. In the basement of my office in Latrobe I have hundreds of club heads waiting for me to put together with shafts and grips. I might get around to working with them someday.

Working with golf clubs wasn't just a function of being a professional golfer. To me it was fun, and I looked at each club I worked on as if I were molding a work of art. Just like my golf game, I was always trying to improve my equipment, too, and that gave me the sense that I was improving on me as I improved on them. I think that is the essence of life—always striving to do something better. Or even perfectly.

HIT IT IN THE HOLE

EVERY TIME I'VE EVER HIT a shot, I tried to hit it in the hole. That includes a tee shot on a par-5. Now, that wouldn't have been very realistic, but that's how I hit every shot in my mind's eye.

I think this might be one of the best thoughts you can have when playing golf, because it really focuses your mind on the ultimate goal. I know over the years it was an effective psychological tool for me. Sam Snead even accused me once of this very thing. I didn't try to dissuade him. That's how I played competitive golf. It was another part of my aggressive identity as a golfer.

There was one important part to my growth as a golfer, and it was this mind-set. When I got out on tour, I was playing a game where I always wanted to beat the ball at the target all the time, but I grew into a player who was capable of beating it at the hole. I went out on tour thinking this way because it was the only game I really knew, and I adapted my game to what I needed to do. But I truly believe I adapted because of how I thought about the game.

You think hard enough about hitting the ball in the hole and you tend to actually do it.

I guess my approach might be akin to Harvey Penick's advice about taking dead aim—with a bit of my own twist to it. Next time you play, let your goal be to try to hit it in the hole. It will simultaneously sharpen your focus and yet free you up to make a swing that is less mechanical or self-consciously driven.

INSTRUCTIONS ON INSTRUCTION

———

I'M THE WORST ADVOCATE for swing coaches, probably, in the world. It's not that I am against instruction, and I think swing instructors are very important to many people starting out in the game. Because of my close association with the PGA of America through the years, I'm a huge supporter of PGA professionals and the important role they play in growing the game and introducing people to playing the game the right way.

But I've never bought into this idea that the young players on the tours need instructional gurus out there helping them, and I am probably least in favor of their growing proliferation on driving ranges at golf tournaments.

All the instructors in the audience will say, "Arnie, stop it" because they're making a hell of a living out of giving instruction. I understand that. I'm not trying to get in the way or impede anyone's ability to make a living. But I think it's gone a little overboard, this babysitting, almost, of a player. And it's not really the instructor's fault. Players ask for the help, and it seems they want their instructors hovering over them.

Every teacher thinks he has the system he thinks is best, and there are so many that you can't count them. But eventually you have to figure some things out for yourself. Is another set of eyes a good idea? I think so. But if you can't go out on the range and make some adjustments on your own, build your own set of fundamentals and depend on yourself, you still might do pretty well, but I would argue that you're never going to be a consistently good player.

Depending on my own system is what carried me through my career. I got that system from my father, who also taught me to drive a tractor and cut fairways at Latrobe Country Club. My father taught me basic fundamentals of the game of golf. The main instruction that he gave me from the day I started playing golf was stick to the basic fundamentals. Like you've heard it a dozen times, when he put my hands on the club, he said, "Boy, don't you ever change that."

Well, basically I haven't. And I think that if you are really serious about playing golf and playing good golf, stick to the basic fundamentals. Sure, there's going to be a little change here and a change there, but you should stick to the things that you started with and you learned and you know how to apply them to your game.

In late 1954, when I left to go on the tour, my father wasn't too anxious for me to go. I said, "I'm going on tour, Pap." He said, "Okay. Be tough, boy. Go out and play your own game. If you start listening to other people's [advice] and all those guys out there, that tractor is still sitting down there and you can drive it when you come back."

Well, I never went back because I did what he told me. Basic fundamentals. If you feel like you're getting the basic fundamentals when you start, and you think you're right and you've got a pretty good swing going for you, stick with it. Don't listen to all the instruction you can get.

My thought always was to create and execute good shots, one at a time. Not perfect swings, but keeping it simple with basic fundamentals that produced the good golf shots, and that served me well.

But I have seen many fellow competitors get twisted into knots, trying new things and searching for that magical swing. In fact, some unfortunate fellows just overthought themselves right off the tour and out of competitive golf. More recently, I have seen what Tiger Woods has done, how he has switched golf instructors a couple of times, and he indeed looks like he's twisted himself into knots. He had such a great golf swing, and while it's easy for me to say he should have stuck with it, I think the evidence is pretty clear that he would have benefited from a bit less intervention from the so-called "experts" out there.

Now, I have had discussions with some golf professionals through the years, and on occasion I have taken something that they have suggested and thought about it and made slight adjustments. But these were things that I did on my own, things I integrated into my own system. I still stayed with my overall fundamentals, and I never had anyone standing behind me critiquing my every swing. It was still my game. As a result, I trusted what I was doing, because it was all on me and I was figuring it out for myself. I think it turned out okay.

JACK

I COULD WRITE A BOOK about my rivalry with Jack
Nicklaus. Inasmuch as there already have been books written
about it, I'll refrain. The attempts to decipher our relationship, break it down psychologically, analyze our words and
body language, have been amusing to me because people con-
tinually are looking for things that just aren't there, that never
have been there.

The facts are fairly straightforward and simple: Jack Nicklaus was my greatest competition in golf, both on the course
during my peak years and off it as our business interests in-
tersected from time to time, most notably in golf course design. Honest and fair competition is a wonderful thing, and
as central to the American way of thinking as anything, and
Jack and I are two intensely competitive individuals who
had the same pursuits and goals in our professional lives.

I liked Jack from the very beginning. We met in Ohio

when he was still a teenager, during an exhibition in 1958 in Athens honoring my good friend Dow Finsterwald. When Jack was thinking of turning pro, he came to me for some advice, and I helped him as much as I could. Some things I told him worked out pretty well for him, and some of the things I told him didn't work out.

I knew how good Jack could be, and I think the world learned that early on when he won two U.S. Amateurs and was my primary adversary at Cherry Hills in the 1960 U.S. Open. When he broke through and beat me in 1962 at Oakmont, the sting of that defeat was sharp. But it wasn't surprising, because he had to start winning eventually. I just wish he hadn't done it in that particular event, in my backyard of sorts outside Pittsburgh.

One of the things that Nicklaus did that was very impressive was that he handled himself very well. He might have made a lot of people mad because he beat me on occasion, but on the golf course he was very good and played the way he wanted to play, and off the course he stayed on the right road and was an exemplary person. We did become friends, and we played a lot of golf together, and we played cards together with our wives, and we traveled together to a lot of exhibitions early on, many times with me picking him up in my plane and taking him to wherever we were playing.

All that being said, there was nobody I ever wanted to beat more, and I think Jack felt the same way about me. Because of that, and because of how we both conducted ourselves throughout our careers toward each other, I think Jack and I have been very good for each other and very good for the

game of golf in general. Our rivalry happened at a time when
golf was just beginning to take deep root in the broader American sports psyche, and the intensity of our competition, as
well as our distinctly different personalities, created tremendous natural drama. The sporting public really took to us.

We knew we were good theater, and we enjoyed it at least
as much as the fans and the reporters. And Mark McCormack,
my good friend and the founder of International Management Group, knew we were good theater, too, which is why
Jack and I traveled all over the world playing in exhibitions.
And each and every time I played against him, whether it
was an exhibition or a major championship, I wanted to
beat him to a pulp, and I knew he felt the same way, and that
always energized the both of us. That's the nature of healthy
sportsmanship and the spirit of tournament golf. That's just
the way it should be, too.

But believe me when I say that despite the pain of losing
major tournaments to each other and the wild swings in fortune that defined our relationship, we had a lot of fun being
in the center of all that attention. And neither one of us ever
lost sight of what it was all about, which was sports and competition, not life and death. That meant that the guy who
lost always was able to congratulate the guy who won with
all sincerity. Likewise, the winner, understanding the disappointment the other man was feeling, was able to be humble
and kind.

I can't think of a better way to behave whatever side of
the fence you end up on in your daily pursuits. And because
of that, we ended up being good partners when we played on

the same team together in the Ryder Cup or Canada Cup. We won the latter together on four occasions, and we also combined to capture the PGA Team Championship three times. After winning the 1971 Team Championship at Laurel Valley by a record six shots in wire-to-wire fashion—one week after my wire-to-wire win at Westchester—I was asked if there was any chance that Jack and I would break up the partnership. "Not so far as I know," I responded. "Why would we do that?"

Were there the occasional moments when we were at odds with each other? I think when two people are friends and yet rivals, there will be moments of disagreement. Like I said, we are very different individuals, but we had one important thing in common: we both benefited from strong father figures who taught us the importance of sportsmanship. I think the fact that we were more than ten years apart in age was a benefit to both of us. And, truthfully, we had not one but two things in common. Each of us married a terrific woman, and Winnie and Barbara Nicklaus became very close friends. They were truly our better halves, and I know Jack would agree with me on this point 100 percent.

So, just how competitive were we?

Let me tell you a story that even Jack has likely never heard. Jack and I both, I think, have been pretty receptive to the idea of signing autographs, even as it has become so much more commercial. I was in Washington, D.C., some years ago, and someone handed me a memorabilia catalogue. I started flipping through it, and I saw that there was a listing for a golf ball, signed personally by yours truly, for $48.50. Well, you probably can guess what I did next. I looked up the asking price for an item signed by Jack. And his golf ball was 60 bucks. I figured, hell, he just didn't sign as many golf balls. But that gives you an insight into our psychology throughout our lives.

To this day we are friends and remain in contact with each other. He and Barbara were there for me when Winnie died, and in 2012, when I received the Congressional Gold Medal, Jack was good enough to attend the ceremony and offer some very nice remarks on my behalf. We have both said this: if one of us needs something, the other would be there for him.

But let me stress this point: from the earliest time in my competition with Jack I thought that our rivalry would last forever. So far, I haven't been proven wrong. And our friendship has stood the test of time, too.

STARDOM

PEOPLE MIGHT THINK THAT "STARDOM," for lack of a better word, was easy for me. It really was not. I never really got used to the idea of being a star, if you will. And then there were the responsibilities that came with it. It was a lot of hard work, a lot of sacrifice.

And I can tell you without hesitation that it was all worth it. Sure, you make sacrifices, but that's simply part of the deal. When you accept all of the accolades and the perks that go with the job, then there has to be something you give up in return. Mostly, it's your time.

I can remember sitting down with Curtis Strange in the late 1980s when Curtis was the top player in the world. I was pretty close to Curtis's late father, Tom, and Curtis, who, like me, went to Wake Forest University, wanted to confide in me the troubles he was having. I was happy to try to help him, but he wasn't having any trouble, per se. He was just finding it difficult dealing with all the responsibilities that came with being a top professional golfer: signing autographs, dealing with sponsors, talking to the media.

After listening to Curtis for a while, I shrugged and told him, "You don't have to do any of that if you don't want to." Curtis was stunned. "How do I not do any of that?" he said.

"Just go home," I told him flatly. "Don't get paid to play golf for a living. Don't take money from sponsors. Don't get paid to wear a shirt or a hat or play with a certain kind of golf club or golf ball. Just give all that back and go home. Then you don't have to do any of that anymore."

About ten years later, when Tiger Woods came along and just swept up the sports world with his talent, he and I had a similar discussion in the champions' locker room at Augusta National Golf Club. "Tigermania" was just beginning. He had a lot of pressure on him, a lot of people pulling him in different directions. He knew I'd understand.

"It's not fair," Tiger said to me over lunch. "I can't be a normal twenty-one-year-old." In short, he resented the obligations of fame. But he sure didn't resent the many advantages and opportunities that came with it. So I told him he was right, that he wasn't a normal twenty-one-year-old.

"Normal twenty-one-year-olds don't have fifty million dollars in the bank," I remarked. "If you want to be a normal twenty-one-year-old, that's fine; just give the money back."

This is a conversation that I've had a few other times since then. I've always tried to tell the younger guys that if they want the perks of stardom, they have to accept the responsibilities, too. Everyone wants to make the money, to be adored and cheered, to be treated special everywhere they go. It's under-standable. It's fun. And it's pretty soothing to the ego. But you can't just go through life taking. At some point you have to give, and what we're asked to give isn't very hard to give. I never found it difficult.

And, frankly, I can't imagine why anyone would find it difficult when the payoff is so enjoyable.

PINE VALLEY

———

I FIRST EARNED MONEY on the golf course when I was eight years old. Because I could hit the ball more than 150 yards in the air, I was presented with a regular business proposition that provided me with a steady stream of movie money. I would hang around the sixth hole at Latrobe Country Club most summer days waiting for a nice lady named Mrs. Fritz, who couldn't carry the irrigation ditch about 100 yards from the ladies' tee. "Arnie," she'd call out, "come here and I'll give you a nickel to hit my ball over that ditch." Over time the nickels mounted up. Big money.

The next time I played golf for any considerable sum—in relative terms—I was the reigning U.S. Amateur champion, and a man in love very much intent on buying an expensive engagement ring for the woman I intended to marry, a girl I had just recently met named Winifred Walzer.

I met Winnie the week after my Amateur victory, when

Fred Waring, celebrated bandleader of the Pennsylvanians, invited me to play in the Waite Memorial at Shawnee-on-the-Delaware. On Monday evening after my practice round I spied two young ladies walking down the stairs of the Shawnee Inn, who it turned out were serving as hostesses for the week. One was Dixie Waring, Fred's daughter, and the other was Winnie, who was unlike any girl I'd ever met, not just pretty and comfortable in almost any social situation, but also smart, well-traveled, and engagingly independent minded. We exchanged pleasantries, and I invited her to come out and watch me play. "Perhaps I will," she said coyly.

We became inseparable for the rest of the week. By Friday night my amateur partner, Tommy Sheehan, and I were leading the tournament. This was quite an accomplishment on my end, because I'll admit my mind was elsewhere, namely on Winnie and how I was going to hang on to her after the tournament. At dinner on Friday evening, sure of the direction I wanted to go, I reached under the table and took her hand and said, "What would you think if I asked you to get married?" Understandably, the question appeared to startle her. "Well, I don't know. This is so sudden. Can I have a day to think about?" she replied.

"Not too long," I said to her. "I've got places to go."

Fortunately for me, she accepted my hasty proposal. To make it official, though, I needed to buy Winnie an engagement ring. But I was only seven months out of the Coast Guard and not making much money as a paint salesman, mostly because I was spending much more time playing golf than selling paint. So money was an issue. My boss in Cleveland, a happy soul named Bill Wehnes, decided to help by making me a deal: he'd pick a par-70 course, and for every stroke under 72 he'd give me $200. A 72 would be a push. But I'd have to give him $100 a stroke for everything over 80. In between I'd get nothing.

It was the kind of bet every friend likes to lay on you: a sucker bet. I'd have to play a great game to make a penny. I'd get nothing for shooting 72 to 79, which is pretty good playing. And I'd have to pay and pay and pay if I had a bad game. But I figured: What the hell; I was young and in love, and what is life like without friends like that?

Then he picked the course: Pine Valley in Clementon, New Jersey, which had a reputation—rightly so—as one of the toughest golf courses in the United States. It was a par-70 layout, but the famed George Crump layout was open for twenty-five years before par was bettered—by 1941 U.S. Open champion Craig Wood, no less. What chance did an amateur have of beating a 72?

"Pine Valley is the shrine of American golf," Ed Sullivan of TV fame once said of the Scottish links–style course, "because so many golfers are buried there."

So this was the course on which I was to "earn" Winnie's engagement ring.

My start was not unusual: I bogeyed the first hole. I also bogeyed the ninth for an outward 36. But I really hustled coming home, and the fifteen-foot birdie putt I made on 18 gave me a 67. In the following two days I shot 69 and 68. Counting side bets and a pretty good run of luck playing gin rummy with Bill and some other friends along for the trip, I pocketed nearly $5,000 that I used to buy Winnie's ring.

A couple of months later I turned pro for real, realizing that my dream of remaining amateur and playing for the United States in the Walker Cup wasn't a very realistic proposition to a mediocre paint salesman with a young bride-to-be.

I think about that weekend at Pine Valley, and it probably wasn't the smartest thing in the world betting money I really didn't have. But it was another marker in my development as a golfer, on the heels of my U.S. Amateur title, that told me I might have what it takes to succeed as a touring professional. Under those circumstances, you sure learn a lot about your ability to play under pressure.

PLAYING BOLDLY

———

PART OF MY "CHARGE" mentality was an unabashed enthusiasm for attempting risky shots. It meant playing boldly. It didn't mean playing recklessly, even if it looked reckless to most observers.

I feel I've never tried a shot that I couldn't make. I relished the challenges, no matter how difficult, but I also understood the nature of the risk and the value of the risk involved.

My first legitimate memory of taking on a risky shot occurred in the Pennsylvania high school state championship at Penn State. Holding a slim lead, I hit a drive into the heavy rough with only a narrow gap through the trees as my avenue to the green. The smart play was to pitch the ball back into the fairway, and a classmate who was serving as my caddie suggested exactly that. But I saw that narrow gap through the trees and there was no way I was going to pitch the ball safely into the fairway. I thought to myself, "That's a shot I think

I can make." So I selected a 5-iron and fired my ball through that opening. The ball landed on the green, just as I envisioned it. A modest gallery was following along that day, and I remember how enthusiastically they cheered that shot. That was quite thrilling to leave observers appreciative of my efforts. And it was personally satisfying to see a shot and pull it off.

And I never really changed the way I approached the game thereafter. Basically, I could not retreat from a challenge. If the chance was there, I was going to take it if it meant winning. And above all I found there was a sweetness in the risks I took while ignoring its dangers. To me, that was the fun in golf. Sure, hitting good, pure shots was rewarding. But recovering spectacularly from poor ones seemed ever more enjoyable to me over the years.

Playing boldly is a philosophy of play, not a style. Boldness doesn't mean playing strictly with power. You can play boldly with chip shots and putts, too. My feeling is that boldness should be a liberating philosophy, not a confining one. I certainly never felt compelled to stick with one style of golf, even if I stuck with one attitude toward it.

I know how to plot my way around a golf course. And I did a fair job of it on many occasions. But all the same I had to inject my rounds with a certain feeling of, well, going for broke. I had to play with a sense of abandon, with full release, with an aggressiveness that was in control, but clearly on the edge. I could never deny my own nature, for I felt like if I was not giving it my all I was not playing to win.

I still recall a time early in my career when I didn't play

with my customary aggressiveness and it proved costly. It was in the 1958 Azalea Open at Cape Fear Country Club in Wilmington, North Carolina—the week before my first Masters win—and I completed 72 holes in a tie with a good player named Howie Johnson. I figured, given my form at the time, that I should be able to beat Howie fairly easily, so I didn't go into our Monday playoff with much fire after lobbying unsuccessfully for a sudden-death playoff. I just wanted to play a nice easy round of golf, with the Masters coming up next. I didn't want to extend myself, exert too much energy. I was out for a pleasant, relaxing round of golf. Bad idea.

Howie played poorly in chilly conditions and came in with a 77. And he won. I shot a 78 that included calling a penalty on myself on the 14th hole when my ball moved on the green. The truth of the matter was that I beat myself by having a different mind-set than my usual aggressive attitude. That cured me forever. I never succumbed again to the temptation of letting down at any time. Howie said afterward that he felt lucky to win with a 77. It wasn't luck; he played better. But my approach to the day was all wrong, and I paid for it.

My belief always has been that you have to play every shot to the hilt, as if your life depended on it. That was my game. And I always found that the harder I worked at the game the more it relaxed me. Furthermore, the minute you stop going for birdies and pars, the minute you're content to get a bogey, something happens to your concentration. You get sloppy in your thinking and the message seeps down into your reflexes. And then you're in trouble, because it is very difficult to get it back.

Some critics have suggested that I might have won another Masters or two and a couple of U.S. Opens had I not played so aggressively. And I have thought that from time to time myself. But had I played less aggressively over the years, it's possible that I might not have won any major titles. I suppose the honest truth is that my playing style probably caused me to lose as many majors as I won. Did I behave irresponsibly? Not totally, because I had something in mind I wanted to do. Am I sorry for what I did? Yes, I am. Would I do it differently? Probably not. It's the way I was, and that's something I have to live with today.

But putting the control of a tournament into someone else's hands and not taking the action of being in control of the situation is much more of a gamble to me. I would rather risk losing any day than lay up and hope for the best.

You either go for the cup or you crawl to it. That's always been my attitude—to take advantage of the tiniest opening to gain an advantage. That's what "go for broke" means to me.

TROUBLE SHOTS

———

THE ENVIRONMENT IN WHICH we learn the game of golf has a lot more impact on how we play the game than people realize. For me, growing up at Latrobe Country Club definitely shaped my strengths and weaknesses.

Because Pap didn't allow the members to practice chipping and putting on the greens, he certainly wasn't going to let me do it, which is one reason my short game was rather weak in my early amateur days. On the other hand, I tended to be perfectly comfortable hitting shots from places where no other golfer ever wanted to be. It turned out to be an important lesson about the game: you've got to learn to live with trouble, and you've got to learn how to get out of it. In golf, as in life, you get some good breaks and some bad breaks, but if you're going to depend on the breaks always going your way, you're in for a surprise.

It's because I practiced so much in the rough when I was

a boy that I developed a realistic attitude toward getting out of trouble. That became my environment. I learned the intellectual process of looking for the various escape routes, of choosing the route that would best serve my purpose, and of picking the club that would help me execute the shot I chose. I believe this was the source of my confidence if I hit a poor drive. I was never fazed by any challenge that confronted me, and I rarely felt mystified by how to rectify the situation and get on the green or at least advance the ball enough to save a par.

Plus, no situation was too daunting to me because of the variety of things I tried. Experimentation kept me busy for hours as a young boy. I remember hitting a ball while standing on one leg and then the other leg, hitting shots with the club turned around or upside down, hitting from pine needles and leaf-covered lies and branches and twigs.

There's a golf lesson in all this, but don't miss sight of the bigger picture, which is that in order to prepare yourself for success, you have to prepare to encounter problems along the way.

PRACTICE

———

IF THERE IS ONE piece of advice I think is the most valuable when it comes to practice, and this applies from the tour professional to the beginner, it's this: know when to stop practicing.

When you have done the work that you needed to do, be satisfied with it, and don't try to finish it off with one more perfect shot. I understand the psychology of it. You want to end on a good note.

The fact is, trying to leave the practice range with a great shot is a great way to work yourself into a rut. You might hit a hook when you didn't want to. So now you want to hit another shot, and it also hooks. Or maybe it slices this time because you have overcompensated. In any event, it isn't what you want to do, either, so you hit yet another ball. The next thing you know, you are wondering what you are doing wrong, leading you to hit another bag or bucket of balls, wearing yourself out and grooving some terrible habits.

It has never bothered me to hit the last shot or even the last few shots badly, not if I have done the right things up to then. If I hit a bad one at the end, my tendency is to consider it an accident. I have known a lot of pros who have to uncork a thunderous drive with their last ball, thinking that's the swing that they will have grooved. But no, it's the total quality of your work in that particular session that matters.

And it's quality that matters much more than quantity. I loved to practice. You can stand at the practice tee and in your mind's eye play an entire round of golf, except for putting, without taking a step. You can concoct a round based on how you hit a shot. Did you pull a driver? Okay, your next shot is a 7-iron from the left rough. Is your "next hole" a par-3? Take a 4-iron and try to stick a shot in there close.

There is nothing better than a well-kept practice area with good rich grass where the ball can sit down just as it does on the golf course, and with big green expanses stretching out in front of you. I call such a place my beautiful green challenge.

I leave this subject with this thought: the harder you work at anything, the more it will relax you. Just make sure the work is productive.

PRESSURE

———

BOBBY JONES SAID that there is golf and tournament golf, and they are not at all the same. The reason they are not the same is because of the inordinate amount of pressure a player endures in a tournament round. And that pressure is ratcheted up to indescribable levels on the final day when you're in contention.

Everyone has a different way of dealing with the tension that can build up as a round progresses and a tournament progresses. For me, I developed a system early in my career, and I played to it. And when I was in trouble or when I was coming down the stretch, I relied on my system. And while I'm not going to get into all the details of the system I used, it all started with the basic fundamentals of the game. And my system dwelled on the basic fundamentals. I relied on my system and I practiced my system all the time. I didn't just go hit balls on the range; I actually worked that system into the scheme of practice so it became a little bit of second nature to me.

Some people might call that a pre-shot routine, which all good players use today, but it wasn't a routine for me in which I had to waggle the club the exact same number of times before every shot. It was more mental approach, a checklist of things I needed to think about before trying to execute.

When you run into a tight spot, a situation so complicated that you're not sure of the way out, that's when you fall back on your system to take you where you want to go. I used my system in each and every game of golf I played.

That doesn't mean that my system left me immune to feeling pressure. Everyone feels pressure, and that's a good thing. I've talked to my grandson Sam about his game after he's played in a tour event, and I have asked him what he might be thinking at a certain time. I'll say, "Sam, what happened? What did you do out there?"

He has said to me, "I got nervous." He was honest about it. He got nervous, and it affected him. Heck, I hope he was nervous, because that's what it's all about. So I have tried to drill in him that you should have a system, but it has to be your system. Play your system, practice your system, and then use that system for every golf shot. I was nervous plenty of times, and I knew that if I weren't nervous I wouldn't be there in the heat of it all with a chance to win. So controlling your nerves is crucial; it is the essence of tournament golf.

Now, I wasn't always able to hit the shots to win. But my system allowed me to be ready to hit the shots. On many occasions, that's what helped me accomplish the things that I wanted to accomplish.

THE DEBUTANTE

———

I ANNOUNCED THAT I was turning professional on November 15, 1954, and three days later I drove myself to Chicago and met with the marketing people at Wilson Sporting Goods Company to sign a contract to represent them that made it official. It was a standard endorsement contract that amounted to $5,000 per year over three years plus a $2,000 signing bonus. Not bad for a paint salesman.

I didn't waste any time going about my business of playing golf. Let me fill you in on my first few weeks after relinquishing my amateur status. Record keepers have me starting at the Brawley Open in Brawley, California, in January 1955, but I got busy much earlier than that.

Three days after I signed with Wilson I played in my first event as a "pro" in Norfolk, Virginia, at Sewells Point Golf Club. I was paired with the club's head professional, John O'Donnell, against former PGA Championship winner

Chandler Harper, a Virginian who played out of Chattanooga, Tennessee, and an amateur from Chattanooga named Ira Templeton. John and I lost the exhibition better-ball match, 2–1, but I shot 68, which was pleasing.

The headlines really blared my name in my first four-day tournament as a professional the following month. Mind you, this wasn't the first time I competed with the professionals. While I was in high school I had a chance to play in the 1948 Dapper Dan Open at Alcoma Country Club in Pittsburgh. Vic Ghezzi was the winner at 17-under 271. I shot a less-than-stellar 306 on rounds of 79-73-76-78.

But now I was a professional, and not some unknown, untested kid from Latrobe but the National Amateur champion. So this is how the national wire report on December 9 from Miami began:

"It's 'Slammin' Sammy Snead against the field today as the $10,000 Miami Open golf tournament gets under way on the palm-lined Miami Springs Course." Later the story informed readers that "top contenders included 13 former winners and most of 1954's major title winners." But there was no mention of Arnold Daniel Palmer there.

Final paragraph: "Snead's strongest competition was expected to come from National Open champion Ed Furgol of St. Louis, defending champion Doug Ford of Yonkers N.Y., PGA titleist Chick Harbert of Northville, Mich., and National Amateur champ Arnold Palmer of Latrobe, Pa., who is now a professional."

Okay, there I was. But it turns out I deserved to be mentioned only in passing because I wasn't very good.

There were 160 players in the field, including ten amateurs. The course had been "stretched" to 6,700 yards. I see these numbers and just shake my head. How times have changed. And then note the purse that year—a whopping $10,000. Bob Rosburg, another rookie, ended up winning top prize of $2,000.

Julius Boros led the first round with a 66. Palmer shot a 69. But that was JOHNNY Palmer. Yours truly, well, his only highlight for two days was getting a ball stuck in a tree and missing just about every fairway for 36 holes to miss the cut.

My official tour debut as a pro in early 1955 went much better. First, though, I played in two unofficial tournaments to try to gather some traveling money for my trip to the West Coast, and it was a good thing I did.

Just nine days after Winnie and I eloped, I competed in the one-day McNaughton Pro-Amateur in Miami. I finished five shots behind Snead, but I still pocketed $520 by tying for second at 2-under-par 70 with Lew Worsham, Claude Harmon, Eldon Briggs, and Joe Lopez Jr. Straight from there I traveled to the Panama Open and picked up another $1,000 for finishing second to Argentina's Tony Cerda. The cash came in handy, because I couldn't earn any money for six months because of the PGA's rules of apprenticeship. Nevertheless, after Monday qualifying at the Brawley Open, I finished 17th with scores of 72, 68, 67, 70.

My tour career had begun. And my lifelong dream had begun to come true.

PUTTING

———

I'M NOT WRITING this book to fill anyone's head with a lot of technical advice. I've written lessons for *Golf Digest* and books on how to play the game. I even wrote an entire book on putting, which is something I'd like to touch on briefly here. Putting is such a crucial aspect of the game because it's the area where scoring largely is determined. I had written earlier about the importance of driving to help set up the ability to score, but putting is where it happens. So if you'll indulge me for a moment, I'd like to share with you one tip that really helped me throughout my career. This is a tip I received early in my career from George Low.

George, who was a fine tour player but made his mark as a putting instructor and designer of putters, was good for me because he used to watch me putt, and he would say to me, "Arnie, you're the greatest putter in the world." Well, as silly as that might sound, that was probably what I needed to hear.

We all need to hear a little pep talk from time to time, and I will be honest: that gave me confidence that I could putt pretty well.

You couldn't have a better friend or bigger supporter than George, and, unfortunately, his enthusiasm got the better of him—and me—in the 1961 Masters. I was on my way to my second straight Masters win and third overall as I marched up the 18th fairway when George, standing by the ropes, called me over to congratulate me. We shook hands. I knew he was excited for me, but the exchange ended up distracting me from the task at hand. I lost my concentration and ended up making double-bogey on the hole to hand the Green Jacket over to my friend Gary Player. As the 1960 winner, that was a tough assignment having to stick around and do the honors for Gary. The kicker was that he won using a George Low–designed putter.

But let's get to the advice you may want to try yourself. I went through a little stretch in 1963 where I was having trouble with some of the shorter putts. Without mentioning my struggles, George said to me, "When you're a little nervous and you're having trouble with your putting, just put your nail of your left thumb in the grip." He wanted me to dig my nail in there and set it in there.

Not too long after that I was playing in the Western Open, and I had about a four-foot putt to win in a playoff against Julius Boros (to whom I had lost in a playoff in the U.S. Open a few weeks prior) and Jack Nicklaus, and I felt kind of shaky. I was trying to get myself in order, and I was going through my fundamentals when I remembered George's advice. I thought, "Well, what the heck, I'll try that." And I put that thumb up and squeezed my nail into the grip and took a few strokes. Then I walked over, eyed the putt carefully, and knocked it in the hole to win the tournament.

SPORT

———

GOLF IS A SPORT—and a darned hard one. And anyone who thinks or says otherwise hasn't competed at the game at the championship level and hasn't been paying attention to the direction of the game today, with many of the best golfers bigger and stronger and more apt to be in the kind of physical condition equal to that of most other athletes.

Periodically, people have tried to make the argument that golf is only a game and not a sport, and, therefore, golfers are not athletes. But for those who play the sport, they have learned that golf might be one of the hardest sports ever invented. The dictionary defines "sport" as: "An activity involving physical exertion and skill that is governed by a set of rules and often undertaken competitively." Yep, that sounds like golf. Now, is it a sport as demanding as football or hockey? Well, no. But neither is tennis or baseball.

Many years back Jimmy Cannon, the great New York

sportswriter, contested the fact that golf should be considered a sport. I contended that golfers have to be fit to play the game and play it well. Being in good shape is an edge for sure. Not long ago Boris Becker, the former top-ranked tennis player, thought golf wasn't very demanding. Then he said he walked for four straight days in a tournament hosted by NBA great Michael Jordan, and that changed his mind: he was exhausted.

But it's more than just being in good shape to handle the rigors of walking 72 holes of championship golf. It's about coordinated strength as well. I certainly played the game with as much athleticism as I could muster because I wanted to hit the ball hard and yet control its trajectory and direction. Jack Nicklaus really brought power to the modern game. Tiger Woods was the best player of his era because he was the best athlete in golf. He could muster incredible power to hit the ball a long way and yet he could be in control of his body and his golf swing, and thus was able to shoot low scores.

Tiger has gone on to inspire a whole new generation of golfers, and just about all of them are bigger and stronger and in better shape. They generate tremendous club head speed, and it's changing the game.

But back to my day. I was incredibly honored to have won the Hickock Belt in 1960 as the top male professional athlete in the United States. The S. Rae Hickok Professional Athlete of the Year Award was created in honor of the founder of the Hickok Manufacturing Company of Rochester, New York, which made belts, hence the choice of a belt as a trophy. It was first awarded in 1950. Ben Hogan won it in

1953, one of three golfers to win the alligator skin belt with the solid gold buckle and decorated with twenty-seven gems, including a four-carat diamond. I was the second, and Lee Trevino in 1972 was the third. Athletes who had won the Hickock Belt include the likes of Jim Brown, Sandy Koufax, Joe Namath, Muhammad Ali, Mickey Mantle, Willie Mays, Bob Cousy, and Rocky Marciano.

I won nine tournaments in 1960, including the Masters and the U.S. Open, and I came within a stroke of adding a third major in a row and having a chance for what I had identified as the modern Grand Slam when I fell a stroke shy of Kel Nagle in the British Open at St. Andrews. I had a good year, but I had never given much thought to how my year of accomplishments compared with other athletes of other sports. I only cared about how much success I had against my golfing peers.

As it was since its inception, the award was announced in Rochester at the annual Children's Charity Dinner of the Rochester Press-Radio Club. I was on my way up to the floor where the dinner was being held and shared an elevator with New York Yankees slugger Roger Maris. After a few seconds, Maris turned to me and asked a little sarcastically, "What the hell are you doing here?"

I knew what he was getting at. Golf isn't really a sport and golfers aren't really athletes. Well, there were eleven of us at that dinner, the finalists who qualified by winning the monthly award as chosen by a group of panelists. The only guy who had won the monthly award twice that year was in that elevator, and it wasn't Maris.

When it was time to reveal the winner, all of the candidates stood up. When they announced my name, I just couldn't help myself. I turned to Maris and said with a smile, "What the hell are you doing here?"

I'd like to think I was standing up for all golfers, not just myself. Later that year I was named *Sports Illustrated* Sportsman of the Year. The defense rests.

TEMPER

———

I'VE ALWAYS HAD A FAIRLY easygoing disposition. But in my younger days you wouldn't have known it if you'd seen me on the golf course. Something significant happened to me in 1946 that really changed how I went about my business on the golf course.

My mother and father were on hand to watch my match in the West Penn Junior finals. At one juncture I missed a short putt, something that infuriated me. (It still does.) In frustration, I flung my putter in disgust over the gallery and some small trees. I won the title, but you wouldn't have known it on the car ride home. I was met by stone silence. Finally, my father spoke up. "If you ever throw a club like that again, you'll never play in another golf tournament."

I knew he was serious. To Pap, there was nothing worse than a poor loser—except being an ungracious winner.

I learned that day the value of never publicly displaying

my anger or frustration—and we all know how frustrating golf can be. The last thing I wanted was to be prevented from playing tournament golf. I gave a lot of thought to what my father said. And for me, the way I decided to deal with some of those frustrations was by talking to people and making conversation out of bad shot.

Was this an act? Not at all. I merely made a conscious decision that I wasn't going to let golf change who I am. It didn't take a lot of effort to simply remember to be myself on the golf course as much as possible. I also took the lessons Pap gave me about good sportsmanship and applied them throughout my career. That way, win or lose, I knew that I was going to do the right thing.

But I still played with emotion. And I let my emotions out on the golf course, but in a much more controlled manner. The gallery still knew I was frustrated if a shot didn't go the way I wanted it to go. In any event, as I became more successful, particularly as a professional, galleries reacted as much to my friendly demeanor as they did to my penchant for wearing my heart on my sleeve. Still, I was adhering to that lesson Pap taught me.

I never threw another club again.

THE CHARGE

THE PALMER CHARGE was a phenomenon that many say was the hallmark of my career, and I would be hard-pressed to disagree. Even if I didn't necessarily pull off as many wins with the charge as people might think, I forged a reputation for comeback wins and late scoring flourishes. Many times I put on a charge that came up just short, but I think that even some near misses furthered my reputation for making a tournament interesting down to the last hole. I know, win or lose, I enjoyed giving it my all.

Ken Venturi once said that we are all chargers out there. He might have been right to a certain degree. Even Jack Nicklaus, as careful and calculating as he was in his approach to the game, knew that there came a time in a golf tournament when you had to try to make something happen if you had any intention of winning.

I explained the mentality of the charge rather succinctly

following my playoff win over Gary Player and Dow Finsterwald in the 1962 Masters Tournament. Trailing Gary by three
strokes after nine holes after an outward 37, I got a much
needed lift with a birdie at the par-4 10th when I rifled a
5-iron to 20 feet and sank the putt. When Gary's approach
sailed long and he missed a six-foot par putt, suddenly I was
behind by just one. I proceeded to birdie four more holes, coming in with a 68 for a three-shot win and my third Green
Jacket. I also erased that horrible memory from the year before when I double-bogeyed the 72nd hole and lost to Gary
by a stroke.

"If I get a birdie at the proper moment just when I need a
psychological lift, then I figure I can birdie them all from
there on," I told the press. "If it doesn't come, you just keep
plowing."

Mark McCormack kept track of my final rounds from
1956 and 1966, and what he found was that when I was in
contention my scoring average was 69.88, while in the same
period my average score per round was 70.57. Somehow I was
able to harness my intense desire to win. The magic year, of
course, was 1960, when I shot 70 or better in the final round
to win seven times, including the Masters (70) and U.S. Open
(65). In the following three years I added another 15 wins with
scores of 70 or lower in the final round. Overall from 1960
to 1963 I won 33 times.

I should point out that I didn't necessarily plan on these
charges. And it wasn't something I necessarily always
relished—unless, of course, I pulled it off. In 1961 I tried to
explain in one golf publication that I would rather not be

known for charging because it's just too hectic. I said that I would rather start off really well. And Winnie even told me she relaxed more when I would start off a round or a tournament with a birdie or a par and get a good start under my belt. But many times I couldn't seem to get my concentration together until the closing moments.

Naturally, everyone thinks of the 1960 U.S. Open at Cherry Hills as the gold standard of charges. Not surprisingly, I would agree. The circumstances are familiar enough by now that I won't recount all the details again, but going out as I did and making birdie on the par-4 first hole by driving to the front of the green was that birdie I needed at that proper moment. In fact, it wasn't just the proper moment, but the absolute crucial moment, for it set up the rest of the round, one in which I had to apply all of my energy and concentration for every stroke.

I still had a lot of energy in the aftermath of what was an exciting day, but I bet there were few nights when I slept better than after winning the national title. I was completely drained. But that's how I knew I had put everything into the charge. And that's what it took to make a charge of that magnitude both in terms of the number of shots I had to make up and the stakes for which we were playing. I'd had other charges before then, but it was not until Cherry Hills that I put the concept of the charge together totally both physically and philosophically.

I must add that I don't think I would have won at Cherry Hills had I not won the Masters two months earlier for my second Green Jacket. The Masters that year validated for me the win at Augusta two years earlier, and the way I did it was important, making two must-have birdies on the final two holes to surge past Ken Venturi. People tend to see the Masters and U.S. Open together only in the larger picture of my going for the Grand Slam that year. But the two championships are much more interconnected than that because the belief I had in going out that afternoon and slugging it out with Cherry Hills was made possible in my mind after my Masters victory. I had proof—very recent proof—that I was capable of doing whatever I needed to do when the pressure was at its highest. Psychologically, the two majors taken together were part of one continuous thought process and spurt of inspiration.

If I was what you might call a "fast finisher," it was because I was always mentally receptive to a fast finish; I was receptive to the idea that there was always time to make up some ground right to the very last hole. I played to win even when common sense dictated that I no longer had a realistic chance. Even when I was playing at my worst or when all the breaks seemed to be going against me, I approached each shot as an opportunity to get going again. That was my golfing personality.

DOWNTIME

———

A LOT WAS MADE out of Tiger Woods taking a break early in 2015 because he was playing so poorly. He said he didn't feel like he was competitive, and he was going to step back and see if he couldn't make some adjustments that would help him play to the level that he demanded of himself.

I fully understood what was going through his mind. And, sometimes, the best thing a golfer can do when not playing well is to take a step back. Frankly, more players should consider it when they are truly struggling. I know it's difficult today when you have world ranking points to think about and the FedExCup Playoffs, but there are times when a break earns you more than another couple of starts would.

In the PGA Championship in mid-August 1969, bothered by bursitis in my right hip, I shot a first-round 82 at NCR

Country Club in Dayton, Ohio, and then had to withdraw. Right then and there I said I wasn't playing again until I felt healthy and was confident I could play golf the way I wanted to play it. I came back in November and won the inaugural Heritage Golf Classic at Harbour Town Golf Links in Hilton Head, South Carolina. The following week I pulled out one of my charges down the stretch and won the Danny Thomas Classic in Memphis.

I bit the bullet again and took time off at the end of 1972 to rest and recalibrate. I wasn't satisfied with how I was playing, so I took a break from the tour and said that I wasn't going to play again until I was satisfied that my game was going to be good enough. And I wanted to make sure that it was good enough not just to compete but to win. It caused me to miss a few tournaments, but I felt that was better than just going out there and building up frustration. That approach paid off when I came out early the next season and won the Bob Hope Desert Classic (as it was called then), shooting 17-under 343 in the five-round tournament to beat Jack Nicklaus and Johnny Miller by two strokes.

It's true that sometimes you have to work things out and play your way through some struggles, but you have to do it in a way that won't compromise your fundamentals or damage your underlying confidence. It takes a lot of strength of mind and discipline, especially when you're a competitive individual, to say that you're not going to play until you feel ready.

In my case, the time I took off did a world of good because

I also was injured and needed to give my body, as well as my game and my confidence, time to heal. When I came back, it didn't take long before I won again at the 1973 Bob Hope Classic, my last regular PGA Tour victory. It sure felt good to prove that I could still get it done.

TOUGHNESS

———

My father's advice about not listening to too much advice had implications beyond simply avoiding the temptation to tinker with the things in my game that worked. I also think he was telling me to be my own man.

During my rookie year I let a fellow professional know that, although I was a rookie, I couldn't be intimidated or let another player dictate how I was going to play golf. At Portland Golf Club, the site of the Western Open, I lost my composure, but made a point.

I was playing with Doug Ford and Marty Furgol in the first round when we came to the 10th hole, a reachable par-5 that I intended to try to get to in two shots. Both Furgol and Ford had played their second shots short of the green while the group ahead of us was still putting. Furgol had a reputation of being impatient, so it was no surprise that he decided to lay up instead of waiting for the green to clear.

As I was preparing to hit, I saw Furgol standing in the middle of the fairway between me and the green. I yelled at Doug to ask Marty to move, and Doug did, but Marty moved only a few feet. I asked Furgol to move again, and he took three more steps to the side, but he was still very much in my line. I had to ask an official to intervene before he finally moved to the edge of the fairway. By now I'm really hot, and I let a good birdie chance go by with a three-putt. Coming off the green I was as mad as I'd ever been on a golf course. I knew Marty had a reputation for this type of behavior, so I let him know how I felt. He feigned innocence, but I said to him, "If you ever pull a stunt like that again I'll take my fists and beat the hell out of you, and if I can't do it with my fists I'll use a golf club."

I think it really shook him up. The truth is, I really wanted to flatten him on the spot, and that really shook me up, too, because I'd never lost my composure like that during a golf tournament. But the upshot was that everyone knew I was no ordinary rookie. I knew how to stand up for myself, and a few years later, in the Masters, I had to stand up for myself again. I'm referring to the 1958 Masters, when I encountered a situation on the 12th hole that could have cost me the tournament if I had not been forceful in arguing on my own behalf in a rules dispute.

The situation came up on the 12th hole of the final round when my tee shot into the green on that tricky par-3 hole embedded into the soft turf just behind the green. I knew there was a local rule in place because of the wet weather that allowed me a free drop, but a tournament rules official named

Arthur Lacey informed me that there would be no such drop given. I knew in my heart and soul that I was right, so I did the only thing I thought I could do, which was play it his way and mine. In the first, I gouged the ball out of the embedded lie and ended up with a double-bogey-five. In the second, I took my drop that I was entitled to, chipped it close, and putted for my par-3.

This left my fate in the hands of the tournament rules committee as to whether they were going to let me have the par or saddle me with the double-bogey. Just to show everyone what I was made of, including Bob Jones, whom I saw riding in a cart as I played my second shot into the par-5 13th hole, I blistered a 3-wood to the back of the green there and made a twenty-foot putt for eagle. Then I parred the 14th. After my drive found the fairway at 15, I was summoned to meet with members of the rules committee, who informed me that they had ruled in my favor. I finished off the round with a birdie for a 73 and 284 total. A dozen golfers were still on the course, but my score held up for a one-stroke victory.

Granted, you don't ever want to be that confrontational on a golf course as I was with Marty Furgol, and I never was again. But I was tough. I knew how to compete. And that served me better in the second instance cited. I had my first Green Jacket to prove it.

TIGER

—————

I FIRST MET Tiger Woods in 1991 when the U.S. Junior Amateur championship was held at my Bay Hill Club & Lodge in Orlando, and I liked the kid and his father, Earl, right away. Tiger won the first of his three straight Junior Amateur titles that year (and six straight USGA championships), an omen if ever there was one as it related not only to his success in USGA events but also in my professional tournament, the Arnold Palmer Invitational Presented by MasterCard.

Five years later, in October 1995, Tiger and I met for dinner when he drove from Stanford University, where he was a sophomore at the time, to Napa, California, where I was playing in the TransAmerica Golf Championship. He wanted to pick my brain about a range of golf-related topics, including the pros and cons of turning professional. I was delighted to oblige, and I picked up the dinner tab, naturally. It was the right thing to do as the elder person, and even though Tiger already was a two-time U.S. Amateur champion and a golfer of renown he was still a college kid.

Unfortunately, that little gesture ended up almost getting Tiger in trouble, because the NCAA has a rule—among many—that prohibits student-athletes from receiving benefits because of their status or reputation. And Tiger was the most celebrated college golfer to come along in decades, having won five straight USGA titles at that point—three U.S. Junior Amateurs and two U.S. Amateurs. (The NCAA also could have penalized Tiger for receiving benefits from an equipment manufacturer, because I had my own club company.) To make things right, Tiger had to write a check to me for $25. Funny, I don't remember whether or not I ever cashed that check. Oh, well, Tiger was off the hook, and thank goodness for that.

Boy, was his mother, Kultida, angry about the NCAA's involvement, telling one newspaper reporter, "The kid was just trying to learn knowledge." I wasn't too thrilled myself. Seemed like an unreasonable rule to me.

Jack Nicklaus and I played a Masters practice round with Tiger in 1996; that's when Jack made his famous declaration that he had just played with a kid who was going to win more Masters than him and me combined (10). The following year Tiger got off to a great start on that journey when he won the 1997 Masters by 12 strokes with a record 18-under-par 270 total.

Many people know that he warmed up for that impressive performance by shooting a 59 at Isleworth Country Club in a practice round with his neighbor, Mark O'Meara. That occurred on a Friday, six days before the opening round of that year's Masters. Isleworth, a par-72 layout in Windermere, Florida, is not far from Bay Hill Club. I designed the course, which opened in 1986, so I certainly knew how good a 13-under-par 59 was on the 7,179-yard layout.

What few people know is that the day before Tiger shot his 59, he joined me for a round of golf at Bay Hill with my business manager from IMG, Alastair Johnston. I like to claim, with a wink, that I helped Tiger warm up for his first major championship win.

Obviously, the twenty-one-year-old Tiger was at the top of his game at that time, but the old guy—I was 67 then—hung in there. We had a friendly little match for $100, and hard as I tried, I couldn't quite hold off a player of that caliber, in his prime—not even on my own golf course. Tiger closed me out on the 17th hole. On the 18th tee, deciding that I didn't want to let Tiger get into my pocket without a last-ditch effort, I challenged Tiger to a one-hole playoff, double or nothing. He readily accepted.

We both hit good drives in the fairway on what is Bay Hill's tough closing par-4 that measures 458 yards and features an oblong green that wraps around a lake. Of course, Tiger was miles ahead of me. I needed a driver to reach the green with my second shot, and I wasn't going to back down. I pulled out the driver. You know: go for broke.

I'll let Alastair tell part of the story from here because I wasn't privy to his conversation with Tiger until much later: "I was standing next to Tiger, and he was really enjoying watching Arnold grinding it out," Alastair said. "He said to me, 'Arnold never gives up, does he?'"

No, I don't. I hit my second shot through the green and into the back bunker, while Tiger found the green with his second shot. I got up and down for a par. Tiger missed his birdie putt, and we halved the hole.

Tiger Woods has won my tournament eight times, tying a PGA Tour record, and it's been a pleasure to shake his hand at the end and congratulate him each time. Tiger and I have had a very good relationship over the years, but I sensed that we grew closer as he got a little bit older. I know when he won my tournament for the fifth time in 2008 we shared a warm embrace, and it felt different than other years. Tiger's father had passed away in 2005, and his relationship with his dad was as strong as mine was with Pap. Perhaps that came through when we shared that hug, and that in some small way he looked upon me as a father figure of sorts.

Nevertheless, on this occasion, he didn't get to walk off the 18th green with more of my hard-earned cash. But he did get a handshake. The following Sunday, he won the Masters.

I'd say that Tiger Woods had quite a couple of weeks of good golf. I'd also like to say I helped by putting him in a good competitive frame of mind. But I think we all know he didn't need my help for that.

WINNING

———

FROM THE MOMENT I turned professional, I suppose you could say that my goal was to win golf tournaments. That sounds like an obvious statement, but bear with me because the concept is somewhat novel given today's environment. I'm talking about a mind-set here.

In those early days the first thing that I thought about was winning tournaments and nothing else. I didn't think about being in contention or getting in the top 10. I didn't care if I was inexperienced or out of my element from time to time. My whole philosophy was based on winning, not finishing a careful fifth. And I didn't care what tournament I was playing in. I played to win no matter what.

Back when I turned professional in 1954, they didn't talk about the majors like they do today. In those days the Masters and the U.S. Open were the primary focus of what you might call "big" events. A lot of people didn't even think about the

British Open and, of course, the PGA Championship. That changed over time, and, yes, I had a little something to do with that. But I remember somebody saying to me, "What are you going to do? Are you going to get really ready for the Masters, or are you going to get really ready for the U.S. Open?"

Personally, I felt that you just win tournaments. Winning the Masters or the Open wasn't the only thing in the world.

Every golf tournament I played in, as far as I was concerned, was a Masters or an Open or the PGA or British Open—and I played them like that. You're playing the same people in the same situations, and I wanted to win those tournaments as much as I wanted to win anything. That was my goal. That was my aim. And nothing was going to get in my way from trying my hardest to do exactly that.

Granted, everyone wants to win or they wouldn't do what they do. But not many people ever think about it. Many times I would think, "I can't lose. I just cannot." Maybe it's an odd way to think, but it drove me to play harder than just "thinking" about winning. Everybody wants to win the tournament, but this "do or die" kind of outlook drove me to accomplish what I wanted and kept me moving forward. I made a lot of golf shots out of desperation, thinking that I had to pull it off because, frankly, I was afraid to lose.

Now, having said all that, you might be persuaded to believe that I was so singular in my thinking that I didn't have any perspective at all about what I considered my mission. But that wasn't true. I still think back to the 1962 Colonial National Invitation at Colonial Country Club in Fort Worth, Texas. In those days I could wrap myself up in a cocoon of concentration, which is important in tournament golf. The secret of concentration is the secret of self-discovery. You reach inside yourself to discover your personal resources and what it takes to match them to the challenge of the game.

At Colonial that year, I was in a playoff with Johnny Pott, and at the ninth hole I found myself in a greenside bunker. I led by a stroke and desperately wanted to get down in two for a par to keep my lead. As I was standing over the ball ready to play the shot, I heard the voice of a small boy behind me. I backed off the shot and laughed as his mother shushed him. Then the boy began crying, so I backed off again. When I settled over the ball a third time, I heard the boy's muffled cry, and when I turned around, there was the little boy turning red because his mother had clamped her hand over his mouth to keep him quiet.

Finally I said to the mother, "Hey, it's okay. Don't choke him. This isn't that important." Then I went back to the ball, blasted out, saved par, and went on to win the tournament.

My good friend and manager Mark McCormack used to say that he thought that episode might have been my finest hour, that another player might not have handled things as well or as coolly as I did, but I was just reacting in a way that fit my overall philosophy. For a lot of players, golf is a way of making a living. For me, golf always has been a way of being alive. And nothing compared to the feeling of going for a victory. I never felt like I had to win at all costs, but I went all out.

LIFE

LIFE GOES ON

———

THERE WERE TIMES I stood on the 18th tee feeling my life would all but end if I didn't win. And when I didn't win I discovered my life, in fact, did not end.

When I lost to Bill Casper in 1966 at Olympic Club in the U.S. Open, it was devastating. I won't try to kid you; it was difficult to stomach, and no setback took more time to shake off. Eventually I did, but it took many weeks of soul-searching and reflection. That final round was one of the most baffling I have ever encountered in my life, but it really reflects what's great about golf. It's amazing how you can just be cruising along and then all of a sudden your game disappears. And when the train leaves the tracks, it's a real struggle to get it back.

What happens is that you let a stroke go somewhere that you know you shouldn't have let go. It might be an easy chip or a putt, what have you. That makes you a little bit anxious, which gets you swinging a bit more quickly. You lose your innate tempo. But, worse, you start thinking quickly. You start pressing, for distance, mainly, but by and large you start trying to hit shots you have no business trying to make.

It's very difficult to reverse your thinking once you go down this road. It's nearly impossible, in fact. You can't seem to find that same frame of mind that made you so comfortable just a few holes before. It happens to even the finest players. It happened to me, and that's how the championship eventually got away from me. A seven-stroke lead with nine holes to play disappeared on me almost in a flash. Bill started playing well at the same time, which contributed further to my anxiety and increasingly poor play. As for the playoff the next day, I tried as hard as I could, but I just couldn't muster any intensity, and my concentration was lacking, too.

Did it hurt? I won't lie; it hurt a lot. When pressed about it, San Francisco was the toughest, given the lead that I had. Especially with my mentality about winning, about feeling that I had to win, losing was a bitter pill, and this might have been the most bitter of all. But as awful as I felt after losing to Billy in that playoff, in many ways my life improved. In the aftermath of that loss, more of life came calling, and I continued on with a slightly different perspective. I was better for the experience.

I was a better person. I had a better perspective on things. I would never have felt good if I had not experienced losing, because losing is part of your life. But there was something else. For quite a few years I had received my share of fan mail, but after the loss at Olympic, the letters were different. People wanted to help. They were comforting and encouraging. It was just a different sensation entirely, and it meant a great deal to me. I looked at everything a little bit differently because of that. I had always appreciated folks, my "Army" of fans, but their gestures of support in defeat meant more to me than any adulation I experienced in victory.

The fans have always been there for me throughout my career. But never were they more helpful and supportive and nurturing—and understanding—than after that time. I'll never forget it, and I still have all those letters today.

ARNIE'S ARMY

————

IT'S TRULY ASTONISHING how something that started so simply and innocently, that started as a seed of an idea expressed in a catchy phrase born of coincidence and circumstances, can be so enduring. And special. And, eventually, so meaningful—especially now.

I'm talking about the phenomenon known as "Arnie's Army."

It was 1959 when I first saw the words "Arnie's Army," but its origin dates to the preceding year when I won my first Masters. Clifford Roberts, cofounder of Augusta National Golf Club with Bob Jones, used GIs from nearby Camp Gordon (now Fort Gordon), the military installation where Cliff spent two years as a young soldier, to man the scoreboards that updated the status of players on the course. (Augusta doesn't use walking standards.) Cliff also gave free passes to any soldier who showed up in uniform. He did the same in

1959. As a former member of the armed services, I can tell you that it felt like my kind of crowd.

A lot of the soldiers did not necessarily know much about golf, but they were fans of this former Coast Guard member, and many of them joined my gallery. That prompted one of the GIs working a back-nine scoreboard—I never learned his name, unfortunately—to herald the arrival of "Arnie's Army" with a handwritten sign, which is what it looked like with all those men in uniform. I can't remember another time, other than my stint in the Coast Guard, when so many uniformed soldiers surrounded me.

A year later, when I won my second Masters title, I thanked the "army" of supporters who came out to follow me. Johnny Hendricks, a sports editor of the *Augusta Chronicle,* picked up on the phrase and ran the headline "Arnie's Army" for the first time. And it stuck. Soon, anyone who occupied my gallery claimed membership in my army, and I was very grateful for that, because so many times throughout my career it was my army of supporters who kept me going and buoyed my spirits no matter how I was playing.

In 1960, during the U.S. Open at Cherry Hills in Denver, the huge gallery was back in my corner like never before as I overcame that seven-stroke deficit to Mike Souchak in the final round. That's still the largest comeback ever orchestrated in the championship. The cheers of the crowd that day will always be among my greatest memories. I truly feel like the support of Arnie's Army had as much to do with my winning the championship as the shots I played.

As far back as I can remember my supporters have been a

great source of strength for me. The fans that I talk to and hear from every day make me want to continue to do the things I do. If you ever get the mail that I get and read the things that people have written to me, it makes me want to continue to play and compete, and I wish that I could—for them as much as for myself.

While I have always appreciated deeply the support of Arnie's Army, I have never quite understood the phenomenon. But I think a psychologist named Dr. Ernest Dichter summed it up best once a long time ago when the Army was really getting into gear. "People see themselves winning through Palmer," he said. "He looks and acts like a regular guy, and at the same time he does the kinds of things others wish they could do. His expressiveness makes his spectators feel that they are part of his game; he looks like he needs their help, and they respond."

I remember teeing off in Palm Springs at the Bob Hope one year in the late 1970s, and because I had a couple of bad rounds, I had to start very early. My tee time was around 7 a.m. Only the mowers were out earlier. But out of the dusk comes Arnie's Army in their pajamas and robes to see me tee off. And, you know, I didn't just wave at the crowd, either; I engaged with them, because I knew many of the people in my galleries so well. At some of these places like the Bob Hope in Palm Springs or Augusta, I not only got to know my fans, but their children, and then the grandchildren.

In recent years, as I have stopped playing competitively, the concept of Arnie's Army is as strong as ever, but it is evolving, and it's something that excites me. We have taken the idea, which is all about support and commitment, and transformed it into a mission to help and cheer on others. I believe Arnie's Army knows that in order to make a better future for all of us, the children need our support. We need to ensure a bright future full of opportunities for all of them.

Golf gave me the opportunity to make a significant impact in the world, to invest in the health and well-being of children. For those of you who followed me during my life, I am eternally grateful for that. But now I hope you will follow me on my next "charge," one that is much more important as we seek to make a positive change in the lives of many people, children especially.

When we sought to create a new charitable initiative, the first thing that came to our minds was Arnie's Army, which conjures thoughts of good folks coming together. Thus, we have started the Arnie's Army Charitable Foundation with a three-pronged mission that puts the community back into community service, as we like to say, by investing in the well-being and development of children, supporting health and wellness initiatives for people of all ages and from all corners of the globe, and strengthening communities and the environment.

All those many years ago an unknown soldier christened my own army for me, an incredible stroke of genius on his part and an incredible stroke of luck for me. And I sincerely hope to pass on that good fortune to children everywhere.

We'd have a slogan that says we are "marching toward a better tomorrow," and I really like that thought. But, frankly, I'm hoping we can charge toward it.

ATTITUDE

————

PEOPLE HAVE OFTEN ASKED ME about the way I have gone about my career, how I have managed to keep a positive attitude, how I have embraced the challenges and so forth, weathered the disappointments, kept moving forward no matter what the obstacles. They figure that it must be hard. Well, the golf aspect of it is certainly difficult. That's the game. And you have to work very hard if you want to be successful. You have to make sacrifices and you have to understand that if you have goals that you want to achieve, there are no shortcuts.

That is especially true when it comes to golf. It is just too hard to take any shortcuts, to think that if you practice just enough that it will be enough. No, you have to go all out. Of course, that's easy for me, as I have already said, because going all out was my style and part of my belief system in how to approach the game.

But the rest of it was really quite easy. And by that I mean that it was easy to have the right attitude because of the way I looked at things.

I am reminded of a Callaway dinner not too long ago at which I was invited to speak. Phil Mickelson was there as well, and we took questions from the audience. A young man asked Phil how he managed to always be smiling on the golf course and to appear as if he was enjoying himself and the crowd. Phil's answer was tremendous. He said, "You do realize that I get to play golf for a living, right?"

That answer was spot on. Indeed, we as professional golfers get to earn a living doing something that many other people elect to do when they go on vacation. So simply start with that premise. We play a game for a living. That in and of itself is a strong reason to have a positive outlook.

Now there are, of course, players on tour who don't necessarily understand this. They know they are fortunate and they are grateful to be making a lot of money playing golf. But do they really embrace what that means? The opportunities before them are truly quite astounding, and I'm not just talking about the money, but also to be doing something that is so enjoyable—playing golf competitively. It's rewarding to your mind and your spirit to be able to travel all over the world to unbelievable golf courses and compete and enjoy those various surroundings.

Sure, the travel can be demanding, and when you are playing poorly it is sometimes hard to remain confident. But that is something else altogether. Even when the game gets frustrating, there is absolutely no reason not to remain positive.

Because the things we get to do, the opportunities that we have, are tremendous. They are the stuff of our dreams.

So when people have seen me out on the golf course throughout my years on tour, they were seeing someone who had a chance to live his dreams. That made it quite easy, whatever the outcome of any tournament, for me to move on and to be eager for the next challenge. To keep all that in mind helped to make it all worthwhile. I don't think I could have had the successes I did have without realizing that. And even though I wanted to win in the worst way, just to have that opportunity was, in my mind, something that was a reward in itself.

To be able to say that I had the good fortune to have it happen to me, I am the most thankful person in this world.

AUTOGRAPHS

———

IF THERE IS ONE DEVELOPMENT in the realm of golf that has been a disappointment to me, it's the nature of autographs.

I have always enjoyed signing autographs, and to this day it's rare that I turn down a request. I have taken this part of my job and career seriously and I try to remain vigilant in reaching out to fans and well-wishers who want my signature on their photos, flags, and other forms of memorabilia. (You'd be surprised by some of the things I have been asked to sign over the years.) In fact, I consider it a privilege to be thought of in such a way that so many people want my autograph. One of my cardinal rules in signing autographs is to make sure that I have a signature that is legible. When they see the signature of Arnold Palmer, they can see that is says "Arnold Palmer" and not some kind of chicken scratching in which some, if not all, of the letters can't be read. I feel so strongly about this that I constantly talk to young players about how they sign their names. Take the time to do it right and with great care. It might take an extra second or two, but it's worth the effort.

I have no idea how much time I devote in a given week to signing things that come into my offices at Bay Hill or Latrobe, but I do know I spend more than $250,000 annually making sure to send it back. It's a small sum in the scheme of things, but I bring it up as a way of giving some idea of the number of items that cross my desk.

What's disappointing is that in the last several years there seem to be more and more people who collect signatures of golfers—and other athletes—for the express purpose of selling them to make money. Even worse, a few years ago Jack Nicklaus, Tiger Woods, and I had to take measures to guard against the counterfeiting of our signatures. And some of these professional signature gatherers even give little kids a few dollars to go up and ask me to autograph something.

I find these types of actions troubling. People are out there subverting the purpose of the whole endeavor, and this saddens me deeply. Is that really what we've come to? And who are these people who want to buy these items, even if they are genuine? Isn't an autograph supposed to represent a personal experience, a memento on which you cannot put a price? It's gotten to where I have, at rare times, declined signing something if I feel it is inappropriate.

Most folks are still very nice in their intentions. And I should point out that I have absolutely no trouble signing something that I know is going to be put up for sale or auction

for a charity purpose. Heck, I'll sign all day for a good cause—
and there are many.

Change happens in one's life, but like some other things
that have happened in my lifetime, this is one change I don't
like. I miss the simple pleasure that used to go with the practice of signing autographs. There was something personally
fulfilling about it for both me and, I hope, golf fans. If I could
go back and fix something in the game, this would be near
the top of the list.

ULTIMATE WIN

———

THE DATE WAS FEBRUARY 22, 1997, and I was standing before a roomful of familiar faces at Bay Hill Club making a few remarks after a dinner following a club function. I knew many of the people in the audience, and their applause as I stepped to the podium was especially enthusiastic.

"I'm here to tell you about prostates," I began. "You know . . . I don't have one."

Roars of laughter followed, and I chuckled myself. But the subject was deadly serious and that's no exaggeration. Only a month earlier I had undergone a procedure to have my prostate removed after biopsy tests revealed what PSA tests had indicated—I had cancer. There were several options available to me, but I was going to make a charge on my recovery by having the thing cut out. And then later I had to endure radiation therapy. As they often say, laughter is the best medicine.

Of course, I had to turn more serious in my remarks. "If

you have a physical, you will want to have a PSA test done every year," I told the crowd. "Believe me, there's someone here that will be affected by this. It could save your life or save the way you like to enjoy your life."

As many people are well aware, you're never quite the same after you've received news of cancer in your life. Before I learned I had cancer, Winnie and I had to endure the endless worrying about our daughter Amy and her own private hell of an ordeal. Fortunately, Amy underwent effective treatments, and today she is cancer free. But there was probably no day darker than the one eighteen months after my cancer diagnosis. That was the day of my last radiation treatment—and on that same day we learned that Winnie had peritoneal carcinoma. Without a doubt that day was the hardest of my life.

The days and weeks that followed were unspeakably difficult. Winnie was the light of my life, my guiding light, the anchor of our family. Losing her just before the holidays in 1999, on Saturday, November 20, was an incredibly difficult time, though the outpouring of love and the tributes to her were heartening and reminded me all the more how many people she had impacted. Her memorial service at the Unity Chapel in Latrobe was a celebration of a life well lived and lived caring about others. I thanked those who came to pay their respects and tried to share what my years with Winnie meant to me. But I didn't have the words. To think that five days after our meeting, the elegant Winnie Walzer agreed to marry this glorified paint salesman says it all about her wonderful heart. My nickname for her was "Win," which could not have been more appropriate.

One of the most touching moments after losing Winnie was the Metropolitan Golf Writers Association creating an award in her honor to recognize an individual in golf who has consistently given his or her time, energy, and enthusiasm to those less fortunate. The first recipient of the Winnie Palmer Award, announced the following June, was one of her dearest friends in the game—Barbara Nicklaus, which I thought was just wonderful, and I felt that Winnie would be as pleased as I was.

It was in October of the previous year that I had revealed to the public Winnie's battle with the disease—during a dinner in Pittsburgh for cancer survivors. As I said before, cancer changes you, and although I already had been involved in various charitable initiatives related to health and medicine, I took an increasing interest in cancer research. Winnie already had a long list of philanthropic interests, including the MD Anderson Cancer Center in Orlando, and soon I found myself immersed in many other projects. Today I am proud of the work we do at the Arnold Palmer Prostate Center at the Eisenhower Medical Center in Palm Springs, California, and at Arnold Palmer Pavilion near Latrobe.

On May 3, 2006, I joined leaders from University of Pittsburgh Medical Center to announce a $2 million gift from the Arnold D. Palmer Charitable Trust to the University of Pittsburgh Cancer Institute. I don't share this for any reason except to highlight how determined I have become in finding treatments for cancer, which is a widespread threat. At the time the National Cancer Institute estimated that more than 10 million people in the U.S. either have had cancer or are being treated for it. The burden of cancer reaches far into our communities and exacts an enormous toll—not just on the patients, but also on families, loved ones, friends, and co-workers.

I am lucky to have survived cancer, but not so lucky to have not felt the sting of tremendous loss in my life due to the disease. This is a fight that I will wage until my last breath, for Winnie, for my family, for everyone who must confront this awful disease.

CIVILITY

———

THE FIRST TEE, which strives to introduce young people to golf, is one of my favorite initiatives for growing the game. But to me it's so important because it's about more than golf.

I have been personally interested in The First Tee from its inception, and I have been excited about its growth. I was delighted to provide the services of my course design company to design one of the early First Tee facilities, appropriately at Augusta, Georgia. I also provided sets of clubs from my golf club company.

The greatest part of The First Tee I learned was its promotion of nine core values: honesty, integrity, respect, sportsmanship, confidence, responsibility, perseverance, courtesy, and judgment. This is how meaningful and positive each of these words are—both their definitions and their golf definitions. To be able to promote these values through golf fits in quite nicely with things I have thought about the game all of my life, and that is that golf can be used to better society.

I would like to restore a kinder, more gentle atmosphere to this world of ours. We will self-destruct if we continue to tolerate such things as greed and arrogance. I can't tell you how supportive I am of one particular aspect of The First Tee. Nothing has gotten me on my soapbox more often in recent years than the erosion of civility and respect in our society. It thrills me to realize that The First Tee is working to correct that.

The breakdown of civility, common decency, and family values is very troubling to me. These are important things. These are the fabric of our country and our civilization.

Whether or not you are a golfer or love golf the way I do, I think we can all agree that promoting what we used to call "good American values" is something we can and should support. As I have gotten older, I feel this is increasingly important. I'm not saying that The First Tee can solve all our problems, but we have to start somewhere, and golf and its lessons are a decent way to go.

THE PRESS

_____

ONE OF THE CONSTANTS in my life that has brought me a fair bit of enjoyment—through all the years of golf, the major championship victories, and the satisfying wins around the world and at home, both amateur and professional—has been the press coverage that I have received. I've enjoyed many of the folks in the press. Some were my friends. I understood their business. They were guys I could talk to and learn things from.

I didn't really pay much attention to the things written about me when I was a young amateur golfer, but I sure noticed a few things after I won the U.S. Amateur in Detroit. I'll never forget that the press was writing some head-turning things, including that my come-from-behind, intense style of play seemed to stimulate the galleries. They noticed how I spoke to spectators and joked with little kids in the crowd, my changing facial expressions as I seemed to react strongly and with great emotion to nearly every shot I struck, the way I hitched my pants as I walked up a fairway.

The truth is I loved these stories, mostly because they confirmed what I dearly hoped was true—that for all my rough edges and lack of refinement I belonged among golf's elite. Jack Clowser of the *Cleveland Press* wrote that "Arnold Palmer was born to be a great golf champion." Not to be outdone, the *Plain Dealer*'s John Dietrich wrote that golf had witnessed the birth of "a new super champion." I still get chills thinking about these stories.

Now, I had enjoyed a fair amount of press since I was a teenager, with my crusty old friend Bob Drum of the *Pittsburgh Press* covering some of my early successes.

I was lucky that newspaper writers took a liking to my style and reported things about me that were quite flattering. Over the years, I enjoyed favorable coverage whether or not I was the winner of this or that particular tournament, perhaps partly because I made myself accessible as much as I could with the media. In the heyday of my professional career, after I'd started to win majors, it was not unusual that I would be summoned to the press center for interviews regardless of my standing in the tournament. I tried to oblige as much as possible.

Of course, there were times when I might have frowned on a particular story here and there, mostly if some particular part of it was inaccurate. But negative press does come with the territory, and there were some stories over the years that were, shall we say, less than complimentary. But I took those in stride. I felt I always was treated fairly, and in return

I felt like the press had a job to do and if I could help them at all, I would.

Only a few episodes have ever made me truly angry. When I decided to promote Callaway's ERC II driver, which was nonconforming to the USGA equipment standards, I was hit pretty hard in some circles. The driver was meant to be used only by amateurs who play casual rounds of golf. I have always respected and dutifully abided by all the Rules of Golf and I have enjoyed a long association with the USGA, including being chairman of its membership program even to this day. I awarded President Gerald Ford the first membership when the program started in 1975. But I also recognized that many amateur golfers didn't necessarily play by the strict rules of golf. They went out and played simply for enjoyment. They took mulligans and gave themselves generous gimmes and didn't count lost balls. A driver that didn't conform to the USGA standards wasn't going to ruin the game, by my way of thinking.

Well, there was a backlash in the media. I was seldom hurt more than when I saw a few headlines calling me "Benedict Arnold." It was unfair and over the line—mean-spirited. It's one thing to disagree on an issue; it's quite another to use your bully pulpit to belittle someone. I don't like that kind of journalism, whether it's being done to me or someone else. That's just one example, and I'll leave it at that.

It would be inaccurate to say my relationship with the media hasn't changed over the years. I used to have great personal relationships with the likes of Drum or Dan Jenkins (now with *Golf Digest*) or some of the other beat writers. We would sit around and BS about things, and we were friends—professional friends. We respected one another and kept many conversations amongst ourselves. But I really can't do that anymore, and I regret having to say that.

Has any of this changed my attitude about the press? Not really. It does, however, change my mind about how I go about dealing with writers today. I still try to accommodate as many people as I can. Doc Giffin, my executive assistant, I think, gets a little more protective of me, and I am more hesitant when he asks me about a prospective interview, but I still want to help the media as much as I can. All in all, they have been pretty good to me over the years.

LIFE JACKET

————

In 2009, I penned an article for the U.S. Naval Institute magazine, *Answering the Call*, which advocated that every person born in the United States should serve his country for at least one year in some fashion—if they are physically able to do so. I feel it should be compulsory. "Such a requirement would benefit both the nation and the individual," I wrote.

There is no doubt in my mind that I benefited from my three years serving in the United States Coast Guard. I became a better person, a better man, and a better citizen. It matured me and allowed me to grow up. I felt like I could handle myself much better emotionally.

I enlisted in the Coast Guard in January of 1951. The country already was engulfed in the Korean War, and joining the Guard was not necessarily a way to avoid danger; the Coast Guard lost a higher percentage of its people in the conflict than any of the other branches of service because its role in escorting ships made Coast Guard vessels primary targets.

I chose the Coast Guard over the other branches because it required only a three-year commitment. It was not a direction I would have ever anticipated going in my life were it not for one of the most tragic things that ever happened to me—the death of my best friend Marvin "Bud" Worsham. It was because of Bud, whose older brother, Lew, won the 1947 U.S. Open, that I had attended Wake Forest University. (At the time, it was Wake Forest College in Wake Forest, North Carolina.) We had met in 1946 at the Hearst Juniors at Oakland Hills Country Club in suburban Detroit, and it's safe to say that we hit it off right away and we became as close as two friends could be. We enjoyed each other's company immensely. Until I met Bud, I hadn't given college much consideration. My family wasn't in the kind of financial position to pay for school. Part of me was thinking I might join the Army rather than wait to be drafted.

Because of Bud's recommendation on my behalf to Wake Forest athletic director Jim Weaver, I was offered the same full ride that Bud had received, and I can tell you that attending college was a fantastic experience, not only because of all the golf that we were able to play year-round in North Carolina, but also because of Bud. But college became torture for me after the events of October 22, 1950.

Wake Forest had defeated Southeastern Conference rival George Washington, 13–0, in the Homecoming Game to remain unbeaten, and after the game we all went back to the Community Club, as the athletic dormitory was called.

I decided to take a nap, but was shaken awake a short time later. Bud said he and Gene Scheer, our neighbor in the room next door, were going to dinner and then a Homecoming dance in Durham, about twenty minutes away. I told Bud that I was planning on going to a movie later with Jim Flick, Gene's roommate.

"Come on, Bud," I said to him, "stay with me. Go with us to the movie." I wish I had been more forceful or convincing, because the next morning I awoke and saw that Bud's bed hadn't been slept in. I went next door and found that Gene had not been back, either.

About an hour later Jim and I were on our way to Durham in coach Johnny Johnston's car. Johnny feared the worst, and to our horror those fears were confirmed when we learned that Bud's Buick had run off the road, hit an abutment on a narrow bridge, and then landed overturned on the rocky streambed, crushing both boys. They were taken to Raleigh, and it was left up to me to identify the bodies when we found the funeral home where they had been taken. It was the worst thing I had ever seen.

Without Bud, being at Wake Forest ceased to have the same meaning for me. He was the whole reason I went there. Jim Flick moved his things into my room, and I finished out the semester, but I realized I couldn't stay there. Of course, Wake Forest has come to mean a great deal to me in the intervening years, but at that time I couldn't stand the thought of being there without my best friend. In 1960, following up on an idea I had not long after Buddy died, I started the Bud Worsham Memorial Scholarship in his honor at Wake Forest.

Among those who attended Wake Forest on that scholarship were Lanny Wadkins, Curtis Strange, and, more recently, Webb Simpson, the 2012 U.S. Open winner.

Against the wishes of my father, I decided that I couldn't return to Wake Forest at the start of 1951 for my last semester. That's when I decided to enlist in the Coast Guard, and I was shipped to boot camp at Cape May in the southern tip of New Jersey. While it was true that I was largely in the Coast Guard to fulfill my military obligation, I took my training and responsibilities seriously. Fortunately, thanks to Pap, the workload, constant discipline, and being chewed out regularly never fazed me in the least. And, as luck would have it, I did get a chance to pursue golf. Well, sort of.

After basic training, the officers at Cape May offered me "permanent party" status. That meant I would stay and train other recruits. I also got another assignment: building a nine-hole golf course on the base in a weed-choked grassy patch of ground located between two airstrips. That was the first golf course I ever designed, and it gave me a real appreciation for the art of golf course architecture. With a rake and shovel I did all of the "design" work myself, single-handedly, and when it was finished I was pleased to see that the officers enjoyed the little pitch-and-putt layout. And I learned a few things that really helped me later when I started designing championship layouts, because I understood not only shot values but also the importance of its care and maintenance.

I was fortunate that I never saw combat in the Coast Guard. After a year I was given an opportunity to transfer to a base of my choice, and I opted for the 9th Coast Guard

District Headquarters in Cleveland, Ohio. In the midst of my last year, as I got a chance to play a little more golf, I won the first of two straight Ohio Amateur titles.

I still keep ties with the Coast Guard, and it's a part of my life for which I am grateful because of the impact it had on me, and that it helped me get through a very difficult time in my life. I think that experience was invaluable, and it prepared me for what lay ahead. That's why I recommend it so highly.

COOLNESS

———

HERE'S A CONFESSION: I never thought of myself as cool, even when people were saying I was cool. How could a kid from simple means who grew up in the foothills of the Alleghenies in western Pennsylvania possibly do anything that was cool? My idea of cool was the hero in a western movie.

I never had a sense of myself as blazing any trails in style or fashion or popular culture. And I never did anything intentionally to seem cool. My mother and father taught me from the beginning that there is no point in being anything other than yourself. People will find you out eventually, and discover who you really are, if you are putting on an act. So I didn't. Now, of course, I always found it fascinating that things that came naturally to me were evidence of my alleged coolness.

Take, for instance, the hitching of the pants. Oh, yeah,

that was cool all right. It was much more cool than letting my pants fall down around my ankles. That's why I did it. I had narrow hips, and so I always hitched my pants to make sure they stayed up. I don't think I caused a revolution in men hitching their pants, though. So how cool was that really? Somehow, people thought it was cool, that it was part of my mannerisms as I was making one of my charges. Honestly, though, because of my experience when I was younger, wearing ill-fitting pants, the hitching became an unconscious nervous habit. Again, I was just being myself.

In 2011, *GQ* magazine included me in a list of the "25 Coolest Athletes of All Time." I'm not sure who was in charge of putting that list together, but it was really quite flattering. *GQ* set the tone of "cool" by beginning the article: "The icons we remember and revere are not always the guys with the best stats or the slickest end-zone dance. They're the ones who played the game like it was an expression of who they were and taught us how to be big-time with grace, style, and swagger. They're the guys we never got tired of watching. And never will."

That was awfully nice. I'd only admit that some of that is accurate as it pertains to me. I've definitely played golf like it was an extension of who I am, that it was part of my identity. It was natural when you're the son of a greenskeeper. And I thought that was cool.

PAP'S AWARD

FROM THE ARNOLD PALMER Regional Airport to the Arnold Palmer Award that goes to the leading money winner each year on the PGA Tour, there are plenty of things out there that, I am honored to say, bear my name. It's all very nice, very flattering, and something that, when I stop to think about it, is very meaningful because of the genuine nature of the gesture behind it.

I can recall one of the best birthday presents I ever received was in 1999 when the Westmoreland County Airport in Latrobe—located about a mile from my home—was renamed in my honor. Talk about feeling overwhelmed.

I was overcome with a similar feeling a few years later when Fred Ridley and some other members of the United States Golf Association informed me that they wanted to rename their museum at Golf House in Far Hills, New Jersey, in my honor. It was a very emotional thing, especially given my long and close relationship with the USGA starting even before I won the 1954 U.S. Amateur. When the Associates Program (since renamed the Members Program) started in 1975, I had the honor, as volunteer national chairman, of giving President Gerald R. Ford the first Associates bag tag in an Oval Office ceremony, which made the president the first official USGA member.

So when the USGA told me about their intention of renaming their historical complex the USGA Museum and Arnold Palmer Center for Golf History, I responded by saying that I had felt like I had won another U.S. Open. It felt that good.

But as special as these things are to me, none of these courtesies even remotely compares—as a matter of emotional effect—to the gesture extended by the PGA of America. That's because it wasn't for me, mind you, but rather for my late father.

In 2014, the PGA created the Deacon Palmer Award to recognize a PGA professional who had to overcome a serious personal obstacle in his or her career to serve the game and the community. My father had polio as a child that left him with a pronounced limp. He wore a brace for as long as I could remember on his left leg. He compensated for this handicap by building up his upper body. He could do several one-handed pull-ups at a time with either hand. My father was tough, and he was smart. That's why, despite his physical limitations, he became not only the golf course greenskeeper at Latrobe, but also, eventually, the head professional.

However, for whatever reason, he was never extended an

invitation to join the PGA of America, or the PGA led him to believe that he couldn't join because of his physical handicap. The circumstances were never 100 percent clear to me, but I know Pap felt slighted by the organization, and this created a certain amount of tension between the organization and me on occasion, though my relationship with the PGA and its members has been a good one over the years. But thanks to Golf Channel president Mike McCarley and former PGA president Ted Bishop, the relationship grew even stronger with the creation of the Deacon Palmer Award. My understanding is that the two men brainstormed the idea together, and then Bishop got the PGA of America board of directors to buy into it.

Ted came to Bay Hill in April of 2014 and informed me of the PGA's idea, and hearing about it brought tears to my eyes, especially when it was further communicated to me that the first recipient of the Deacon Palmer Award would, in fact, be Milfred Jerome "Deacon" Palmer. That November at the PGA Annual Meeting in Indianapolis, I accepted the award on my father's behalf.

It was a big day for both of us.

DREAMS

I DREAMED THAT ONE DAY I would be the star in a western movie, which would have fulfilled a childhood ambition of mine. Oh, yes, I often pretended to be the cowboy riding to the rescue, the guy in the white hat who would vanquish the bad guys with six-guns blazing. Not surprisingly, I have loved watching western movies all my life, and once provided *Golf World* magazine with a list of my favorites. As I recall, most of them were John Wayne films.

After my cameo appearance in Bob Hope's film *Call Me Bwana,* I had some serious conversations with Jay Michaels about producing a feature film with a western theme. Jay had been our producer for *Challenge Golf,* and we explored the possibility more than once. But it always seemed to get pushed aside for some reason or another—mostly golf, not surprisingly. Then in the early 1980s Jay passed away suddenly, and

Mark McCormack, my business manager, who worked closely with Jay on *Challenge Golf,* never really pursued it in earnest, and I didn't push the idea very much.

I'm a dreamer. I freely and readily admit that. But I consider that one of my strongest qualities.

I don't hope for things, or rather I don't hope certain things happen to me. To hope is to wait for things to come to you. To dream is part of the process of setting goals and then striving to achieve them. You first must dream of doing things before you can do them.

When I was preparing to play in my last Masters in 2004, I was asked about how strong was my desire to make the cut. I hadn't made the cut in the Masters in several years, and I said that it was very important to me to try as hard as I could to play all four rounds in my 50th and final Masters. I think some of the writers were having a hard time understanding my thought process.

I simply explained that I knew myself well. I think my actual words were that "I've been associated with me for a while." Not a bad line. And I continued by talking about being a dreamer. There are not many people who recognize that quality in themselves or want to recognize that quality in themselves. I was always a dreamer when it came to my golf, and I think that was one of the secrets to my success, but it applied to other things in life, too. That's the way I thought and the way I felt, so that's the way I lived.

When it comes to golf I still have dreams. I'm eighty-six as of this writing, and my shoulder is banged up and my back is giving me trouble, but I still want to go out and try to hit a golf ball as well as I can. Not every dream that I've ever had has come true, but a lot of them sure have. So I believe in the power of dreams. I sure would have enjoyed filming that western, though.

FATHERHOOD

———

NOTHING IN MY LIFE has been more rewarding than being a father, and perhaps nothing has been as challenging, either, particularly when you're a father who traveled frequently on the job and had to contend with some of the pressures and perks of fame.

Winnie and I raised two beautiful, intelligent, creative, strong-willed daughters. I know that Peggy and Amy got the beautiful, intelligent, and creative part from their mother. It's beyond words describing how proud I am of them, the kind of good-hearted person each is, and how genuinely decent and down-to-earth they always have been.

When I think about how they had to grow up, I realize how difficult it was for them being the children of Arnold and Winnie Palmer. They had to deal with a lot of things going on around them, and they faced challenges a lot of other children didn't have to endure.

They attended a private school, but that was not our original choice for them. Winnie and I didn't want to spoil the girls or to have them feel more privileged than any other children, so we were dead set that they were going to attend public schools, and they started out at the local grammar school. Unfortunately, they did get that sense that they were somehow different—but not from their parents. Other kids knew who they were, what their father did, and they, therefore, felt inclined to treat them often not in a manner that was nice or polite. They faced their share of rudeness to the point we had to place them in a private school where few cared about their last name.

Even so, the girls worked jobs throughout their high school and college years. We wanted them to earn their own money and learn how to work, just as Winnie and I had from our respective parents. While they were attending college, neither Peg nor Amy had the benefit of a personal car, and Winnie and I insisted that they were going to get an education and learn to do something with their lives.

There was no getting around the personal and financial advantages the girls were going to enjoy, but they handled it all very well. I'd like to think that Winnie and I provided the proper direction, but my daughters didn't let themselves get caught up in the trappings of their circumstances. They grew up to be solid citizens and kind, giving, strong women—just like their mother. And it pleases me greatly to see each of their children grow up to be a good person with fine personal qualities. For instance, I felt proud to hear that my grandson Sam, who has played in the Arnold Palmer Invitational Presented

by MasterCard a number of times, acted in a cordial, respectful, and mannerly fashion toward his amateur partners in the
tournament's pro-am. That is much more rewarding to me
than how he scored in the tournament proper.

It's not enough to simply provide the basic necessities and
maybe some creature comforts to your children. A parent
needs to offer strong direction in attitude and behavior, which
I can say my parents did for my siblings and me. Being a parent isn't easy, as anyone with children is well aware. But like
golf itself, it's not supposed to be easy. It's a challenge, one
that needs to be met with intelligence and strength. Good
parenting is the most important endeavor a person can under-
take. But the rewards surpass anything else you do in life.

FLYING

———

I'M ASKED OFTEN what I would have done with my life if I hadn't become a successful professional golfer. It's a difficult subject because golf has been such a thorough and essential part of my life. I will say it again: golf, for me, always has been a way of being alive.

Something that has come a close second is flying. So when the question is asked, my response is that I would have become a commercial pilot. Other than the amount of time I have spent on the golf course or with my family, the happiest hours of my life have been spent in the left seat of an aircraft.

I learned to fly a Cessna 172 single-engine plane not long after I turned professional and could afford to take flying lessons, and by 1958 I was flying myself to many of my tournaments, exhibitions, and other business responsibilities in a leased Cessna 175. Learning to fly and then owning my own planes, starting in 1962 with an Aero Commander 500, a secondhand aircraft for which I paid $27,000, was a real game-changer in my life. I discovered a tremendous sense of freedom in flying myself. No longer was I beholden to airline schedules or limited to major cities. The planes I flew took off when I was ready for them to leave and could fly into any town that had an airstrip. If a tournament finished late, I didn't have to wait until Monday morning to return home; I could fly myself home Sunday night in time to kiss my girls good night.

In short, I found I was more productive in my professional life and was able to get more enjoyment out of my personal life by having more time with the people who meant the most to me—my wife and daughters and my larger circle of family and friends.

Two early experiences in flight shaped my future as a pilot, one exhilarating and the other frightening.

The first occurred when I was thirteen years old, when a family friend named Tony Arch took me up in a J-3 Piper Super Cub, a high-wing two-seater. Tony had washed out of fighter pilot school at the onset of World War II, but he still had his pilot's license. I quickly learned a bit about why he washed out. As we made one of several low passes over the golf course, he nearly stalled the plane by pulling back on the stick without giving the throttle enough power. We're lucky we didn't crash, but the tail rudder did scrape a portion of one of the fairways. I thought it was exciting.

The second came in 1949 when I was on a commercial DC-3 from Chattanooga, Tennessee, on a return trip from an amateur event. We encountered a ferocious thunderstorm.

The plane was struck by lightning, sending a ball of static electricity (known as St. Elmo's Fire) hurtling down the aisle. It really terrified the passengers, including this one, who was twenty at the time. Later, after thinking about that event, I realized that flying was something I wanted to learn more about. Not long after I turned pro and could afford the lessons, I set about doing just that, taking instruction from Babe Krinock at Latrobe Airport.

I went on to own eight airplanes, including my current one, which is the second Cessna Citation X I purchased and the fastest private jet of its class in the world. I averaged more than 200 flight hours per year, and I've traveled more than two million miles by air. And though I stopped piloting my own aircraft in 2011, I am still logging the miles in my plane with the call letters N1AP—November One Alpha Papa. By the way, I also became licensed to pilot a helicopter.

While there have been many highlights to my golf career, I've also enjoyed a few landmark moments in the air, most notably in May 1976 when we set a round-the-world speed record in a Learjet that still stands for planes in that classification. With me were two other pilots, Bill Purkey and Jim Bir, plus journalist Bob Serling, and we set off from Denver and then flew to Boston, Wales, Paris, Tehran, Sri Lanka, Jakarta, Manila, Wake Island, Honolulu, and back to Denver in 57 hours, 25 minutes, and 42 seconds. It might have been faster, but we had to make an unexpected stop in Wales for fuel, and in Sri Lanka, on another refueling stop, I rode on an elephant. We departed Denver Stapleton Airport at 10:24

a.m. on May 17 and buzzed the tower at Denver at 7:49 p.m. May 19 to signal the end of our journey. Another highlight was flying a Boeing 747 before they were even in commercial service. Not long after I jumped at the chance to do the same in a new DC-10. On several occasions I had the privilege of flying with the Blue Angels, the U.S. Navy's precision-flying jet squadron.

In 1996, my longtime friend Russ Meyer, who had moved on to head up Cessna, flew the new Citation X into Latrobe with his wife to pick up Winnie and me. We made a hop straight to St. Andrews, where I was granted membership in the Royal & Ancient Golf Club of St. Andrews.

I could go on and cite dozens more. Pap always instructed me to keep my feet firmly planted on the ground, but it's been in the air that I've enjoyed many of the most satisfying times of my life. Strangely, perhaps, some of the most soul-soothing moments have come after some difficult setback on the golf course. To be able to get in my plane, soar into the wild blue yonder, get my mind off worldly problems, and just enjoy the ride and the feeling of ultimate freedom was reinvigorating. Many times, by the time I landed the plane at home, my disappointment had usually dissipated. Its therapeutic value to my mental well-being was immense.

It's hard for many people to believe how I turned an innate fear into one of the most rewarding and gratifying things I've ever done in my life. Sometimes, when I think of it that way, I find it a little hard to believe myself. But that's how it all came together. Getting out of your comfort zone, or in this extreme case, facing circumstances that are frightening, more often than not is one of the best things you can do in your life. Taking that first step can be hard, and maybe it doesn't turn out as rewarding as it turned out for me, but to my way of thinking, it sure beats living in fear.

HEROES

————

MY FATHER WAS MY HERO, and there was no one
else who was a close second in terms of inspiration or influence.

But there were definitely people that I looked up to and
who did have an impact on me in my career, starting with
Bobby Jones. Around the time I was ten or eleven I began
reading books about golf and picking up ideas here and there.
I was naturally drawn to the exploits of Jones, and a biogra-
phy I read about the great amateur had a profound effect on
how I thought about what I wanted for my own career. Certainly his capturing the Grand Slam of his era—the U.S. and
British Opens and Amateur championships—got me thinking
about what would constitute the modern version, which I
began talking about after my wins in the Masters and U.S.
Open in 1960.

And, of course, Jones continued to be an inspiration as I
got to know him better once I won my first Masters in 1958.

What Jones accomplished in the creation of Augusta National Golf Club and the Masters Tournament is something that had a profound impact on me from the very first time I visited in 1955. Beyond that, Jones's courage and dignity in battling that debilitating disease that eventually ended his life in 1971 was truly amazing.

Because of his flair and style, I put Walter Hagen high up on my list of people in the game who had an impact on me. I didn't style myself after Hagen in any way, but I appreciated how he went about playing the game and enjoying it along the way, and that is one thing from Hagen I tried to emulate. I first met Hagen at the 1955 PGA Championship at Meadowbrook Country Club in Detroit. We hit it off pretty well, and from time to time we'd talk. It was always a nice conversation. We'd talk about my golf, we'd talk about his golf, we'd talk about what was going on out on the tour. We had a lot of common interests, and we found that we were fairly like-minded about the game.

When I won my second consecutive British Open at Royal Troon in 1962, Hagen was kind enough to call me in Scotland to congratulate me. We had a special relationship that I enjoyed immensely. When he died in 1969, I served as one of the pallbearers at his funeral in Michigan, as he requested. That was a huge honor.

The gentleman I held in perhaps the highest esteem of all was Byron Nelson. His writings, his ideas about the golf swing, and the way he came up through the caddie ranks to be one of the greatest players in the history of the game all made an impression on me. Some of the things I did with my golf swing, trying to keep it on plane, those came from Byron Nelson. They worked well for me for a lot of years.

That we would become friends was something that was very special to me. You can talk about his great swing and the eleven tournament wins in a row in 1945, but the thing that impressed me the most was that he was simply a fantastic person. He did nothing during his long life but make great contributions to the game and to life itself.

I don't think I've ever been more flattered in my life than when Byron introduced me during a banquet in Dallas and said that, "Arnold has meant more to golf than is really possible to say, especially professional golf." I was speechless that Byron would say something like that about me when I had always revered him so highly and considered him such an important figure. I guess we were members of the mutual admiration society. It also touched me deeply that he would call me one of his dearest friends. Then he added, "He did the foreword for my book [*How I Played the Game*] and I know that sold a lot of extra copies."

Byron's passing in 2006 was very difficult for me. I felt like not only myself but also the whole world had lost a great friend. But I was better for having known him personally, and the value in that is beyond the bounds of expression.

SOFT SPOT

WHEN WINNIE AND THE GIRLS and I started to settle in at our new winter home in Orlando, there were many people who helped us feel comfortable and welcome. Folks were incredibly nice and cordial, and that was one of the primary reasons why we loved it so much.

One of the most important and, as it turns out, influential people was Frank Hubbard, an Orlando businessman, who was involved with the Florida Citrus Open and who was really the force behind my decision to agree to host the event at Bay Hill starting in 1979. A few years later Frank was instrumental in getting me involved in something that has become a very special part of my life. He wanted me to lend my name and financial support to something many folks believed was greatly needed in the Orlando area—namely a first-rate children's hospital.

Children are my soft spot, and I was happy to do whatever

I could. But I soon decided that I needed to jump in with both feet and use whatever clout I could muster to make a bigger impact after we toured the cramped, outdated children's wing of Orlando Regional Medical Center. Meeting the courageous children battling cancer and other diseases and seeing so many tiny, frail premature babies on life support touched a nerve like you wouldn't believe.

Quickly, we were able to increase the goals of a fund-raising campaign from $10 million to $30 million, and players like Greg Norman and Scott Hoch helped raise awareness and offer financial support. Winnie was instrumental in our decision to make the children's hospital the principal beneficiary of charitable proceeds from our PGA Tour event at Bay Hill.

I had quite an emotionally charged sixtieth birthday, but only because of the days leading up to it when we opened the Arnold Palmer Hospital for Children and Women. We celebrated a ribbon cutting on August 26 and enjoyed hospital gala activities that day and the following. Even greater was the opening of the Winnie Palmer Hospital for Women & Babies on May 25, 2006. Just six days later, the first baby was born there.

Today, the Arnold Palmer Medical Center that incorporates the two hospitals is the largest facility in the U.S. dedicated to children and women. Naturally, I am very proud of my career record as a golfer, to have realized the kind of success that I dreamed of when I was just a child. But a legacy of helping children means so much more to me.

IKE

——————

ON MARCH 8, 1990, I received a letter from U.S. senator Bob Dole formally requesting that I make a speech before a joint session of Congress. The occasion was the 100th birthday of the late Dwight D. Eisenhower on October 14. I've delivered a lot of speeches in my life, but none on so momentous an occasion or so special to me. There was pressure like I had never felt before. It was an important speech, and I couldn't take my usual approach of simply jotting down a few reminder notes and then speaking to a crowd like I would to guys in my foursome.

I couldn't do that this time. I knew that my remarks would be aired on C-SPAN and preserved forever in the Congressional Record. Doc Giffin, Winnie, and I spent hours putting together a compilation of stories and memories I had of President Eisenhower. There were so many.

I enjoyed great relationships with a number of U.S. presidents and played golf with many of them, but none of them compared to Ike, who was kind, charismatic, and unpretentious while possessing a strong presence. Before I ever met him, I had been fascinated by President Eisenhower and his distinguished military career prior to his becoming the thirty-fourth President of the United States.

I met President Eisenhower a few months after my first Masters win in 1958 at Laurel Valley Golf Club in Ligonier, Pennsylvania, a club that I helped start and which I represented on the tour. A mutual friend, Ben Fairless, the former chairman of U.S. Steel, introduced us, and we shook hands and spoke briefly. I wouldn't learn until a bit later that Ike was an avid golfer and was responsible for a putting green being installed on the White House grounds not far from the Oval Office.

Some months after that meeting I received a letter from the president on his own personal stationery that really floored me. The letter read, in part, "Because of the general confusion the other day, I failed to realize when Ben Fairless introduced us that you were Arnold Palmer of 1958 Masters fame. I hope you will forgive my lack of reaction and accept, even this belatedly, my warm congratulations on your splendid victory."

The president, a member of Augusta National Golf Club, suggested we might try to play together there in the future, but the occasion wouldn't materialize until after my second Masters win in 1960. A deep and meaningful friendship was born, one that I cherished increasingly in the passing years.

Though I never felt more comfortable around anyone of that stature than I did around Ike, I have to admit I was still in awe of him.

We played plenty of golf together, including his only public outing at Merion Golf Club in 1964 for the Heart Association of Southeastern Pennsylvania, and I enjoyed those times immensely, but I savored more our private conversations when we would talk about the tour or I would pepper him with questions about his military service or current events.

Our most memorable conversations were the private ones we shared in 1966 at my home in Latrobe when he surprised me for my thirty-seventh birthday. After Winnie had kept me busy most of the morning with piddling chores, a family friend dropped by, and as we started talking about my plane, a Jet Commander, the first jet I ever owned, I noticed a plane overhead that looked a lot like mine. Turned out that it *was* mine, with the president inside. A few minutes later there came a knock on the front door. President Eisenhower stood in the doorway with a small overnight bag in his hand. "You wouldn't have room to put up an old man for the night, would you?"

I had planned to play golf that day, but this was a much more appealing option, spending the weekend with Ike. Mamie Eisenhower came in by car a little later (she had a fear of flying), and the four of us enjoyed a wonderful time together. Ike presented me with an oil painting he had done of a field and barn on his farm in Gettysburg. I still have the picture hanging in my house and consider it my most prized possession. It was a terrific present, but even more special to me was simply sitting and talking with him on a range of topics. During our talks, he ended up sharing some very private concerns he had on some weighty matters. I haven't forgotten what he told me, but I've never repeated our conversation to anyone.

I was more than happy, however—deeply honored, really—to share many other stories about President Eisenhower during my speech to Congress. I was as nervous as I had ever been when the sergeant-at-arms recognized me and I made my way to the podium. Ike had stood there many times to give his State of the Union address. It was an intimidating environment, but thinking of my friend helped me relax. I was able to get through the speech without referring to my prepared notes very often. I merely told as best I could the stories of my friendship with the president and what kind of a man he was. He truly was a great man and a great American, and I was blessed to have known him.

I think he knew that I felt that way. I believe that that is one of the great gifts we can give to our friends—letting them know how special they are.

GOLF AND MY GIRLS

——————

I ALWAYS WANTED my two daughters, Peggy and Amy, to play golf, but I never wanted to push them into it. I didn't feel that was a healthy or helpful thing to do; Winnie and I felt they should take a natural interest in it. And they did, which pleased me tremendously. Peg was about seven and Amy five when they really started to play a little, and truth is they benefited as much or more from lessons Pap taught them than anything I tried to teach them.

My desire for them to play golf was not so they could follow in my footsteps or their grandfather's. I just felt it was important for them to be introduced to a game they could enjoy their whole lives and be active in a pursuit that is healthful and teaches a young person poise and confidence and patience. Golf is a clean game that can give a youngster an opportunity to discover that work and determination will produce improvement and success. You don't need anyone else around to "compete" at it. You're playing against yourself, really, as well as the golf course, and that also allows a youngster time to figure things out for himself or herself, to experiment, and to feel the fulfillment of hitting a few good shots all on their own ability.

Plus, it's a game that the whole family can enjoy together. I thought that was very important.

The best thing a parent can do is not force their children into golf. This just hurts them and hurts whatever curiosity they might have in the game. But if they show some interest, try to provide them some opportunities for exposure, even if it's a few holes here and there. And a few lessons would be crucial.

But don't coddle children and try to help them too much. Winnie and I bought the girls their own sets of clubs, but we insisted that they carry their own bags, to walk the course, and to keep their own scores accurately and honestly.

It's important, however, to hold off on any expectations for your children. I didn't with mine. Winnie and Pap and I all took a reserved approach to what the girls were doing. They received a golf lesson only when they asked to have one. And they could stop when they wanted. When we were out on the course, they didn't have to finish a hole. They could stop whenever they got tired or their hands got sore. Pushing a child to keep playing when they are tired can lead to poor swing habits, frustration, and resentment of the game.

Over time the girls learned to play a little and developed a healthy interest in the game by following along in my gallery. And some of their children play the game, too. That's been another source of pride. Most notably, Amy's son, Sam, won the club championship at Bay Hill and has gone on to become a solid professional golfer on the PGA Tour, and Peggy's son, Will, also has a lot of talent, winning the club championship at Latrobe, and plays golf at Loyola, Maryland.

I think our whole family has had a lot of fun in the game. And I have had a wonderful time watching my family enjoy it.

KIT

———

BETTER LUCKY THAN GOOD. So goes the saying about golfers. Well, I would have to agree, because I have been about the luckiest man who ever lived, at least when it comes to my personal life and finding not one, but two of the most wonderful women with which to share my life.

Winnie Walzer was the absolute love of my life, and our nearly forty-five years together were nothing short of magical, starting with the first time we met. If I can claim to be smart about anything, it's that it took me less than a week to ask Winnie to marry me, and losing her in 1999 still is a painful thought. Of course I still miss her, and I always will.

But I thank God that in my later years I have had another terrific lady by my side. Kathleen (Kit) Gawthrop did me the honor of marrying me on January 26, 2005, at a private ceremony at Turtle Bay Resort in Kahuku, Oahu, Hawaii, where I was to play in a Champions Tour event later that week. It was a Wednesday afternoon, and there were no witnesses beyond Pastor Ron Valenciana and a cat that wandered onto our porch. My chief pilot, Pete Luster, and Cori Britt, my VP of Arnold Palmer Enterprises, who was serving as my caddie that week, joined us later for a small celebration.

I had known Kit for decades, having met her socially when her father-in-law was part of the ownership group at Pebble Beach early in my career. Several years after I lost Winnie, Kit and I became reacquainted, and it was a very important thing for me to be able to spend time with someone close to my own age who likes the things that I like. A California native, Kit had been divorced for twenty years when we started "dating." Once again I was smart enough to realize that she is the kind of person who is thoughtful and giving. And fun. In short, she's a gem.

It's nice to be able to pick up the phone several times a day to call her and share some news with her, good or bad, and later at home to enjoy dinner or watching sports on television or just talking. Her companionship is a soothing blanket of comfort as I have slowed down—although I haven't slowed down too much. Another great thing about Kit is her patience, as I have stayed pretty busy.

And there is one more thing about Kit that is truly endearing, and that is her absolute acceptance of everything that already was in place in my life, including the fact that I will always miss Winnie and hold her in my heart. But I hold Kit close in my heart, too. How can you not love a woman who says that she in no way feels she lives in Winnie's shadow, as she told one reporter not long ago. "I think it's nice to see how

Winnie is still ever-present in Arnold's life, where she lived and the influence she had."

Kit has three terrific children and eight grandchildren to blend with my two daughters and six grandchildren, and we enjoy that part of our lives as well, having a big family to look after. As I write this, Kit and I are going on our eleventh year together, and it's been a blessing having her in my life. You bet I'm lucky, and I wish for that kind of luck for everybody.

LATROBE

———

I HAVE GOTTEN THE QUESTION a lot over the years: why I choose to come back to Latrobe in the spring and stay into October, and the answer is actually quite simple. It is my home, and by that I mean that it isn't just where I came from and where I grew up, but it's the home that's in my heart. If there's one thing I've learned in all these years, it's this: your hometown is not where you're from, but it's who you are.

You tell me a place that is nicer than Latrobe. You can't. There isn't another place like it. It's perfect. That's how I see it. Now, of course, I have my home in Florida. I love being at Bay Hill, enjoy Orlando, and during the heart of my competitive career there were practical reasons to have a place in the southern U.S. where I could work on my game and prepare for the next season. I have a lot of special associations there that are very important to me at Bay Hill, including the

PGA Tour event that I host and the hospital, to which I have devoted a lot of time and energy.

But I'll always have Latrobe. I'll always be from Latrobe. I look out from my home now and I can see the house I grew up in. It's gone, but I can see it in my mind's eye and feel the love of my mother and father and smell the air of the golf course, and that takes me back to my youth. You can't replace that. You can't replicate it.

The idea of "home" for me isn't just a single structure where I eat and sleep. It's a total environment. It doesn't have much in the way of luxury, but it does have what I want most: convenience. For instance, from the front door of our house, it is 100 steps to the front door of my office, just one minute down the road from Pap's old house, two minutes to the first tee of Latrobe Country Club, and just four minutes from the airport. Literally everything I need to fill my life—golf, family, friends, and flying—is only a matter of seconds from my front door.

Furthermore, the place is history in itself as I see it. My history. When I learned to shoot a shotgun, my father and I walked that hillside right there and shot pheasants and rabbits and squirrels, and took them down and cleaned them in the stream right over here about 200 yards away. And my mother would put them in salt water overnight, and we'd have them the next day.

When I was about seven or eight years old, an old oak tree toppled over on the course. The trunk had rotted and honeybees had moved in. The trunk was full of honey. It was something seeing those honeycombs. Pap said to me, "Now, Arnie, we're going to take this honey home, and give it to your mother, and we're going to eat it. But before we do, we've got to get two five-pound bags of sugar. When we take the honey out, we're going to put those two bags of sugar right there, so the bees can have their food." So that's what we did. My father was wise in so many ways.

I've had contracts slid under my nose that were quite lucrative. Country clubs came calling, asking me to be their touring professional, but the stipulation many times was that I had to set up some kind of residence near the club. They couldn't pay enough, and I turned them down without a moment's hesitation or regret.

What's home? Home is the place you return to after losing the 1966 U.S. Open in devastating fashion and feel the love of your friends and neighbors. I attended a country club dance the week after losing that playoff to Bill Casper, and the members treated me as if I had won. Home is where I can go play eighteen holes of golf, and the only attention I'll receive for most of that round is a wave from a friend or acquaintance.

There's another old tree on the golf course, just off the left side of the 18th fairway, that was turned into a sculpture of my father, an idea my brother Jerry conceived and implemented. More poignantly, when my father and mother passed away, we had their ashes spread near the 18th green. And when Winnie died in 1999, her ashes were spread on another part of the old course. You can probably guess where I will end up someday. (I once joked that I didn't want to be buried in a cemetery because I had no interest in hanging around a bunch of dead people.)

We all have to recognize where we are from. It's a big part of who we are. Wherever that is, it's important to embrace it. That's not to say every person has to go back and live in his or her hometown. That's not the point. The point is to take that place and the best memories of it and go forward with your life recognizing that it's been integral to who you have become. It should be a great source of happiness. I know it is for me. And I know it's one reason, probably the biggest, in fact, why I have always lived quite happily.

MANNERS

I'VE HEARD IT said by several people over the years, and PGA Tour commissioner Tim Finchem has been one of them, that my rudder is pretty well fixed and steady, and that you won't find me deviating from some established norms and traditions that I believe in. I find this one of the nicest compliments that I could receive, because I believe it's good to respect traditions, manners, and the finer points of social grace, because it simply makes life more pleasant for everyone.

I believe that you really show respect for others by adhering to certain proprieties.

As an example, I don't find it polite for men to wear hats indoors. My father was a stickler on this, among many things he thought were important, including little details like how to hold your fork or knife properly. And God forbid if you dared enter a dwelling or be in the presence of a woman and forget to remove your cap. Pap would snatch it off and take part of your scalp with it for such a transgression. You learn pretty quickly right and wrong when you have a strong figure teaching you the ropes as forcefully as Pap did. Obviously, many of those lessons stuck, because I think that's disrespectful to wear hats indoors, and I make it a hard and fast rule that hats will be removed once a gentleman enters the clubhouse at Latrobe Country Club or at Bay Hill Club & Lodge.

I have other expectations of my fellow man that I myself practice. I can recall meeting a young and upcoming player at my tournament at Bay Hill Club a few years ago. Tim Finchem introduced us. The young golfer was sporting a scruff of hair on his face, which I realize is considered stylish today though it's not for me. I found him a pleasant young man, but I thought his appearance was not very professional.

After a few minutes of light conversation, we shook hands and parted company. I made sure to tell him as he left that I expected him to be clean-shaven when I saw him out on the golf course for the first round of the tournament.

The next day, as I was out cruising around in my golf cart watching the golf, I came across that young man. As I got a bit closer, I noticed that he was clean-shaven. It brought a smile to my face.

On a more recent note, my business advisor, Alastair Johnston, pointed out how times change. Just last year at the British Open at the Old Course at St. Andrews, I was lingering with Alastair in the R&A clubhouse commenting on the beard David Duval was sporting and that I thought it was not becoming of an Open champion to have facial hair. Alastair wheeled his gaze around the room at the portraits of past champions like Old Tom Morris, Willie Park, and others. Of course, they had healthy facial hair. I had to laugh at the irony. But let me point out that shaving wasn't exactly as easy or convenient then as it is today. That was the style of the day.

From all this, you might get the impression that I'm a pretty strong-minded person and maybe a bit stodgy. I am, and I don't think there is a thing wrong with that. I get it from Pap. But I got something else from Pap, too: to do things well for their own sake and never compromise on that.

MOM

I HAVE WRITTEN QUITE a bit about my father and the impact he had on my life, but I'd be remiss in not pointing out how much my mother influenced me.

I owe my first playing experiences on a golf course entirely to Mom, and I probably owe my personality to Doris Palmer, too. One of five daughters, my mother was a classic "people person" interested in just about everyone and what they had going on in their lives. She took a genuine interest in friends and neighbors and even people she had just met. She was magnetic and charming, and nobody ever had a bad word to say about her. People were drawn to her, perhaps because she was consistently upbeat and filled with generosity.

She was encouraging and nurturing, and she certainly knew how to be welcoming to people of all walks of life. Our house near where the old sixth hole used to be located seemed to be a gathering spot, particularly in the winter when folks would be out sledding down the hill from the seventh hole. I think these kinds of experiences were critical to the formation of my attitudes about life and meeting people. In some ways, she was a complete contrast to my father.

But Mom, just like Pap, had a lot of common sense, and she always was there for me with a lot of good advice. One piece of advice that still resonates with me has to do with walking, which was great because it fit well into my life as a golfer. If you played golf, you walked, and even when Pap, grudgingly, started offering carts at Latrobe Country Club, my attitude was pretty well fixed because of Mom, who encouraged me to walk just about everywhere that I could. She maintained that walking every day was about the most important thing someone could do.

I was conditioned to walk my whole life not because of golf but because of school. When I was six years old, I started going to elementary school in Youngstown. That was the fall of 1935. It was a mile one way, and I walked to school and back every day by myself until my sister started going, and then I walked with her.

I was honored to serve for twenty years as honorary national chairman of the March of Dimes and its work with dealing with birth defects and its battle against polio, and because of what my father went through with polio as an infant, that was something that really touched a nerve in me, and I wanted to help. It felt like the appropriate thing to do, considering we raised millions annually with walkathons and that I participated in several Walk America events in Washington, D.C., that helped further raise awareness and money.

A good, long walk is good for the body and it really clears the mind. You can do a lot of good thinking on a long walk. I can remember many wonderful walks I had out on the golf course. I know that sounds a little out of character for me, but many mornings I started my day by going on the golf course without my clubs and stretching my legs.

The habit of walking has stayed with me my whole life, and I would venture it is one reason for my generally good health throughout my career and my longevity.

OAKMONT

———

THE REPUTATION OF Oakmont Country Club, near Pittsburgh, was something I was aware of at a fairly young age. It was the gold standard of private golf clubs and the course was known as one of the most difficult in the world.

The club came to mean a great deal in my life. I played my first U.S. Open there in 1953 and my last in 1994. In between, I had two very realistic chances to win the national championship there, in 1962, of course, and again in 1973 when Johnny Miller shot that brilliant final-round 63 that stunned us all.

But there actually was a time when the club had the potential to play an even larger role in my life. I remember Pap coming to me while I was working on the tractor, and my first thought was, "Oh, no, what have I done wrong now?" I was still just a kid. But when I stopped the tractor, Pap came around the side and said, "Arn, you'll never guess what just happened." He went on to tell me that he had an opportunity to take the job as head greenskeeper at Oakmont. Well, that got my attention. My eyes got real big. I was thinking, "Wow, wouldn't it be something to get to play golf at Oakmont Country Club all the time?"

Pap had to tell me to slow down, that he didn't know what he was going to do, and anyway, there wasn't a guarantee that I was going to be playing Oakmont all the time. He could say that, but I knew better, because I knew me.

He thought about it for three or four days and then he came back to me and told me that he had decided that he couldn't take the job at Oakmont and he was going to stay at Latrobe Country Club. There were several reasons, but none more important than the small-town life we were living. We had family and friends around and it was really a perfect situation from about every angle. Then there was the fact that Oakmont hosted major tournaments. While hard work never bothered Pap, he didn't want to be working more than the fourteen to fifteen hours he already was working at Latrobe, and missing even more time away from his wife and children.

He asked me if I was disappointed, and I tried to hide the fact that I was a little disappointed. But there were sound reasons for his decision, and I agreed with all of them.

I have never really given that episode much thought since. I wouldn't trade anything for my life experiences at Latrobe. And who's to say that my game and my life would have developed the way it did? Things do happen for a reason and work out for the best. You might not see it right away, but they become clearer in time.

PRIORITIES

———

KNOW YOUR PRIORITIES. Know them and live them and you'll be surprised how much you can accomplish, how much time you have for things you don't think you have time for, and how fulfilling your life can be.

I always knew what was most important to me. When I was growing up, nothing was more important than golf, but that's the attitude of a young person who hasn't a care in the world. Later on I figured it out. Family was first. Always. Then golf and business come after. We all get put to the test on this, and occasionally we have to make allowances here and there, but I can tell you, that's not something you want to make a habit.

Milton Richman, the great UPI wire service sportswriter, wrote a story about me that illustrates what I'm talking about. I had no idea he was writing the story, and I was a little embarrassed when I read it recently. It was 1971, and I had just won the Westchester Classic in Rye, New York, by an easy five shots in wire-to-wire fashion. I was pretty excited about the victory. So was Winnie, and she couldn't wait to talk to me, so she called the pressroom at Westchester Country Club. She mostly talked and I mostly listened, having no idea that anyone was paying attention to a forty-one-year-old man talking to his wife on the telephone. That's not exactly breaking news.

But then things got a little more hectic for me. There was another call that had come in, and the locker room attendant had picked it up. The man on the other end of the phone said he wanted to talk to me and that he was the President of the United States. At first the club employee didn't believe him, but eventually he recognized the voice of Richard Nixon.

Nixon was an avid golfer, but he hadn't played much while in office. He was calling to congratulate me on my third win of the year, and he also hoped to learn to one day hit a bunker shot like the one I hit on 16 in the final round that turned out to be one of the keys to my win. It was a nice phone call. I didn't find all this out, however, until I was finished talking to Winnie. The locker room man tried to get my attention, and after a few more minutes, one of the reporters slipped a note in front of me that read, "President Nixon is on the phone." I nodded, but Winnie had a few more things to tell me, so I stayed with her. It was more important to make sure things were right in my house before the White House.

When she finished and said her piece, I told her I had to go take another call, not letting on until later when I got home who the other person calling was at that time.

I had no idea Milton was observing these goings-on, but there it was in his "Sports Parade" column the next day. It was a very nice story and quite flattering, but, like I said, I was a bit embarrassed reading about what a swell guy I was. I only tell this story now to make a point, not to tell you what a swell guy I am.

I enjoyed the victory that day, but it was special because I still had a chance to share it with Winnie, even if it was on the telephone. Look, even the President of the United States has to wait when something more important is going on in your life.

STAYING GROUNDED

————

My dad never stopped giving me guidance about how I should look at my life and career. By 1961 I had already established myself as a perennial winner and a major champion with two Masters titles and the 1960 U.S. Open.

But my father was determined that no matter how much I won, how successful I became or how much I earned, he wanted me to remain humble. He wanted me to stay grounded and to focus on my work and not get too caught up with all of the accomplishments.

One of the best lessons he ever gave me came after I had won the 1961 British Open at Royal Birkdale. I had been dining with dukes and princes over the course of an entire week and came back to the United States the conquering hero. Naturally, I was feeling pretty good about myself.

When I got back to Latrobe, I was very excited about my victory and the chance to share it with my family. My dad greeted me with open arms. I could see how happy he was for me. But in his second breath he said, "Now, why don't you put down that Claret Jug. I need your help mowing the back nine."

Looking back, this was a very important marker to me. It reminded me that if I'm going to be successful, I must continue to grow with a balance of confidence and humble appreciation for all the people involved in making it possible. If I didn't understand where I had come from and how I had gotten there, then the chances were I was not going to be as successful going forward. And I would certainly not have the proper attitude about how to live my life and do the right things.

Did I mow the back nine for him? You bet I did. And do you know what? There was a certain peace and serenity in doing such a familiar, simple task. It was satisfying in its own way. Looking back, it was a rather appropriate way for me to celebrate winning the Open Championship.

THE INTERVIEW

My LONGTIME EXECUTIVE assistant Doc Giffin likes to tell a flattering story about me that occurred long ago at the Western Open in Chicago. I hope today's professional golfers might take away something from this anecdote, which is the reason I want to share it with you and why I think Doc enjoys it so much.

I was in the tournament pressroom at Medinah Country Club conducting a post-round interview with a group of reporters. At the time Doc was working for the PGA of America as the tour media official, and when I finished up with the press, Doc asked me if I had time for a radio interview.

I said, sure, and soon up steps this young college kid who was working as an intern at one of the local radio stations. He looked very nervous, but we got through the interview, which lasted nearly ten minutes, just fine. At least I thought we had. I started to get up, and I noticed that the young man's face was beet red. He had forgotten to turn on the recorder. Well, I couldn't just leave him there without the interview, so I said "It's okay, son. Let's do it again," and sat back down and did the interview for the second time.

Doc tells the story because he has spent a great deal of time around professional golfers, first in his duties with the tour and later as my right-hand man, and he wonders how many other players, past or present, would be as understanding about the young man's plight.

In my mind, I don't think what I did was particularly special.

Bobby Jones once said about being complimented for calling a penalty on himself that, "you might as well praise a man for not robbing a bank." In other words, Jones didn't think he should get credit for doing the right thing. By the same token, I don't deserve any special commendations for simply helping someone, or in this case, doing a little extra for someone who made a simple mistake. I never gave it a second thought. But that's how I was raised—you put yourself in the shoes of the other person.

You might think that there's nothing in it for me to have such an attitude. Since when does there have to be something in it for you to treat people with the same respect you would want bestowed on you? But having said that, I felt that I did get something in return. I got peace of mind. That's a pretty valuable commodity.

HEEEERE'S . . . ARNIE

I HAVE NEVER FORGIVEN Spiro Agnew for stealing my thunder on national television. Especially when television had been so good to me over the years.

On Friday, July 17, 1970, I sat in for Johnny Carson as host of NBC's *Tonight Show,* and in addition to tennis great Rod Laver, the Vice President of the United States joined Johnny's regular sidekick, Ed McMahon, and me on the popular television talk show. We taped the program in the afternoon in New York, and it aired that evening. Boy, was I nervous, much more nervous than on the first tee of any golf tournament I had ever played.

My anxiety level, I suppose, was quite understandable. If you are put into a situation that is foreign to you, then of course you're going to be anxious. I'd played golf in front of thousands of people and millions at home watching on television, but that was totally different. Golf is something I've been prepared to do since I was a kid. And I'd joined Bob Hope on some of his TV specials, but my lines were scripted, and I also knew I could rely on Bob if there were any glitches.

In addition, under terms of a deal with NBC that was finalized in 1967, I also was contracted to provide television analysis of various golf broadcasts. Again, that was an arena in which I was comfortable. I knew a little about golf. I made my debut that September for NBC's coverage of the World Series of Golf in Akron, Ohio, joining Jim Simpson. I wish I had been playing, but some guy named Jack Nicklaus edged me in the U.S. Open at Baltusrol, so, even though I was the No. 2 money leader behind Nicklaus that season, I didn't qualify for the sixth edition of the event that featured the four major winners playing for $50,000. As an aside, Jack was asked on the eve of the tournament what he thought of my moving into the broadcast booth. My good friend replied, grinning, "I think that ought to be a permanent job for him."

The Tonight Show, on the other hand, was real pressure, because it was all on me as the host. But not too long into the show it became all about Vice President Agnew, who was quite funny. He had come prepared, too, carrying two golf clubs and a tennis racquet with him onto the set. Earlier in the year, playing in the Bob Hope Classic Pro-Am, Agnew had hit Doug Sanders in the neck with a stray shot. As for the tennis racquet, Agnew recently had made more news for hitting a playing partner with a serve in doubles. "I brought my weapons with me," he said immediately, making fun of himself.

"I like to get out and play golf and tennis," he said. "It gives me a chance to apologize."

And he continued with this during our time together, telling the audience that President Richard Nixon doesn't make fun of Agnew's golf, "he just keeps a respectful distance."

I got in on the act, showing photos of the vice president and me playing golf in Florida. "Here we are teeing it up," I said, "and watching the Secret Service run for cover."

The various reviews of the program the next day were very complimentary . . . toward Agnew. I guess that's what a good host is supposed to do—facilitate great answers from his guests. I don't understand why I was never asked back to do it again.

BE YOURSELF

———

I MADE MY FIRST of many visits to the White House in early 1969. The date was February 13, a Thursday. President Richard Nixon hosted Green Bay Packers quarterback Bart Starr, Detroit Tigers slugger Al Kaline, and me as we visited the nation's capital for a dinner for the National Press Club's Sports Night. The three of us were on a national tour as part of what was called the Lincoln-Mercury Sports Team.

To say that I was more than a little nervous is an understatement. The thought of a small-town boy from humble beginnings going to the White House generated a feeling of excitement mixed with awe. How do you even prepare yourself for something like that? In my case, I went back to the fundamentals. Just like I did on a golf course, I had fundamentals off the course, too. Just try to be as natural as possible, be polite, mind your manners.

Of course, that's all I ever tried to do is just be myself

in every situation. That usually worked—most of the time, anyway.

I found President Nixon to be a congenial guy, who really enjoyed sports. During that visit we "swapped yarns" as they say, and when we posed for a photo on a sofa in his office, he said, "I always like to sit with a bunch of champions." He and Starr were particularly friendly, since it was the Packers QB who helped Nixon win the Wisconsin presidential primary.

I had my moment when I was asked to hit a few golf shots into a net. Kaline, who was a good friend, asked me for a golf tip. Al wasn't a particularly good golfer, and he wondered how he could improve. I couldn't resist a smart-aleck response. "Stay off the golf course," I advised him. He laughed, accepting the dig in the spirit it was intended.

Later in the year, on December 20, I attended my first gala dinner at the White House, this one a Christmas celebration. The president called on me to make some extemporaneous remarks. Suddenly, the steak on my plate looked like a cold plate of beans. I took the opportunity to needle Nixon about inserting himself into the debate over who ought to be the No. 1 college team in the nation. The president had asserted it ought to be the Texas Longhorns, while Pennsylvania partisans, including me, thought unbeaten Penn State ought to be ranked first. "I'm honored to be among such a great football expert," I began.

Amazingly, I was invited back. Perhaps because I was being myself, and because I did mind my manners, for the most part.

WINNIE PALMER
NATURE RESERVE

———

In 2001 I purchased an undeveloped twenty-six-acre tract of land near Latrobe that offered sweeping views of the basilica and campus at Saint Vincent College. It would have been a great business investment, as I am sure that I could have parlayed the purchase into commercial development, having seen it happen with a large parcel of land near Route 30 and Route 981, next to Latrobe Airport and not far from my home.

But I bought it for the express purpose of making sure that didn't happen, something I did as much for the community as for my late wife, Winnie. Instead, we've been able to transform that property into the Winnie Palmer Nature Reserve, which has come to represent many of the things that Winnie held dear and cherished in her life and in this community that she grew to love as much as I have all my life.

Anyone who knows me is aware of my appreciation for the natural wonders of the world, but Winnie might have had an even greater appreciation for nature. Winnie had served on the board of directors for Saint Vincent, and she had regularly expressed her love for the parcel of land that was available for sale from two local families. Having seen how the community received the aforementioned development, Winnie voiced her concern to me that the same thing could happen to this piece of property and potentially ruin the beautiful view of Saint Vincent College and Archabbey across the open fields.

We incorporated the Winnie Palmer Nature Reserve in October 2000, less than a year after she had passed away, and Saint Vincent Archabbey donated an additional twenty-five acres adjacent to the property, a historically intriguing piece of land, as it turns out, as it was crossed by the British Army during the Revolutionary War. Now it's used for hiking and recreation as well as conservation and environmental education. People can hike more than two miles of trails, and enjoy the various plantings, including an area to raise crops for research, and a diversity of wildlife and wetlands.

A barn purchased by the monastery in 1919 and used for storage was moved and serves as the Environmental Learning Barn. Winnie would have loved that; she had an appreciation for barns, and she convinced me to purchase and refurbish a barn near Latrobe Country Club that truly enhances the landscape. A stone patio behind the Nature Reserve barn is at the base of the natural amphitheater and features an abstract sculpture designed by artist Julie Amrany of Chicago to reflect Winnie's love of nature and reading. (She also was a longtime supporter of Latrobe's Adams Memorial Library.)

It meant a lot to me that we were able to get all of this done, and that we could do even more thanks to my good friend Tom Ridge, who as governor of Pennsylvania helped with the development of the land through a $500,000 grant that was part of the state's $30 million "Growing Greener" program, the largest in the history of the state for environmental purposes.

Since the very beginning of this project I have proudly served as the board chairman, and it has been a very emotional thing for me to see what we have been able to do as a community to preserve such a special piece of land. I just know that Winnie would have approved of all we have done.

I can't conceive of a better tribute to her memory.

BUSINESS

McCORMACK

———

MY CLOSE FRIEND and business advisor Mark Mc-Cormack passed away on May 16, 2003, but his influence on my life and career is still indescribably significant. Other than my father and Winnie, no one had a bigger impact on the direction of my life and the conduct of it than Mark did, and while I miss his wise, no-nonsense counsel, I miss his friendship even more.

I met Mark in 1950 at a college golf match in Raleigh. He was the No. 2 man for William & Mary, and I only have a vague recollection of that meeting, which was no more than a passing handshake; I didn't play against him that day. Our paths didn't cross again until the 1956 Masters, and it was not a chance encounter; Mark came up to me on the putting green the morning of the first round and delivered a putter from Bob Toski that Bob had used to win the 1954 World Championship at Tam O'Shanter in 1954. We exchanged a few pleasantries, and then he was on his way while I finished 21st in my second Masters.

Two years later, after he graduated from Yale Law School and was working as an attorney at the firm of Arter, Hadden, Wykoff & Van Duzer in Cleveland, Mark, a pretty fair golfer who competed in the 1958 U.S. Open, hit upon an idea to start another company called National Sports Management, Inc. The goal was to represent golfers in booking golf exhibitions. Mark had convinced Toski, Gene Littler, and a few others to join his enterprise, and that fall he arranged a meeting with a group of other players in Atlanta. Among those who went to hear what Mark had to say were Dow Finsterwald and me. I had won my first Masters earlier that year and Dow had captured the first PGA Championship contested at stroke play. We liked what we heard, and Mark arranged a few exhibitions for me in 1959 for fees ranging from $350 to $500.

At the end of the year Mark and I had a conversation that changed both our lives and the larger world of professional sports. I had found myself faced with more business opportunities that I didn't have the time or expertise to delve into properly. I asked Mark if he would manage me exclusively. We shook hands and off we went.

Well, that's the myth. What really happened is that Mark balked at the idea, admitting there were areas of the golf/business world about which he knew little, and he wondered if his NSM company couldn't better assist me. But I was insistent that he work with me exclusively. It was not an easy decision for Mark. He was also representing a score of other good players, including Art Wall, who won the 1959 Masters, and Bill Casper, who won his first U.S. Open that year. Fortunately for me, Mark agreed to my request, and we shook hands on a deal that was our bond until the day he died. Years later I reluctantly allowed Mark to add a few more clients, and he started with Jack Nicklaus and then Gary Player. He branched out from golf after that to sign Jean-Claude Killy, the alpine ski racer, and Jackie Stewart, the Formula One racing driver.

In 1961 we formed Arnold Palmer Enterprises to better handle the myriad opportunities that were now pouring in after my 1960 season that included my victories in the Masters and U.S. Open. And soon after that came the birth of the famous multicolored umbrella, our signature logo, which we wanted to use on clothing, business stationery, golf clubs, and other items related to the business. I hit upon the idea after an unexpected source of inspiration during a brainstorming session at the Holiday Inn in Ligonier, Pennsylvania, one rainy day. We were struggling for inspiration when I looked out the window and saw a woman get out of her car and open a multicolored umbrella. Fortunately for us, Travelers Insurance, which also used an umbrella logo, hadn't locked up the entire umbrella category. So the open golf umbrella done in four colors—red, green, yellow, and white to signify the various components of our company—became a worldwide symbol for Arnold Palmer and his business ventures. To further differentiate it, we had the umbrella tilted to the right.

Back to Mark and me. The two of us proved to be a great team; we complemented each other. Mark was simply a brilliant person. In some areas, he lacked maybe some common sense as far as how to make certain deals work, and I did offer that bit when it came to marketing situations in golf.

As our success grew, naturally Mark became a more sought-after business manager—he disliked being called an agent—and he created International Management Group, with Gary Player and Jack Nicklaus among the initial additions in his stable. The Big Three was born, and IMG was on its way to becoming much more than just a management company for a few golfers but rather a worldwide conglomerate representing athletes in all sports as well as artists and entertainers. In the mid-1970s, as Mark built IMG into the giant of representation it is today, he assigned my affairs to a talented and savvy Scotsman named Alastair Johnston, who has been a trusted advisor ever since.

As time passed and we both got increasingly busy with our own lives, Mark and I drifted apart. There were times when I felt he wasn't living up to his end of our handshake bargain, and I wrote more than a few pointed letters telling him just that. But these were letters I never sent, remaining in something I called my "X File." In the end, I never left IMG out of a deep sense of loyalty—and a deep sense of friendship that never waned even if we saw less of each other. Mark, who in later years was ranked by various media outlets as one of the top five or ten most powerful men in sports, never flinched from standing beside me during some hard times, and he was instrumental in so many of the great things that occurred in my business life.

Occasionally I felt stretched a bit thin, but that was my choice and not something that Mark was responsible for, except that he was doing his job finding and creating opportunities for me. And his decision to have Alastair looking after me still is a source of comfort and exemplifies all that was good about Mark, for he knew how to size up people and make good decisions on my behalf.

On January 16, Mark fell into a coma four months before his death after suffering a stroke stemming from an adverse reaction to anesthesia, which had been necessary for an outpatient surgical procedure. The news was devastating. I had just seen him days earlier at our traditional breakfast meeting we enjoyed together every January. I was at Bay Hill when word reached me, and I was just about to head to Palm Springs and then eventually to Hawaii for the Senior Skins Game. Mark's medical condition weighed heavily on me throughout that trip. I could not believe something like that could have happened to him, and, sadly, his condition never improved.

When Mark died, it was only natural that the press wanted my reaction and a few words. Those words didn't come easily, and trying to sum up what Mark had meant to me was impossible. But I tried, and I leave you with the words I chose then: "I have lost one of my closest friends, and the world of sports and entertainment has lost one of its giants. I never had a moment's regret or misgiving about placing much of the guidance of my future in his hands, and it certainly proved to be the right thing for both of us."

VERSATILITY

————

IF I COULD PICK A year where my golf and business seemed to be riding a crest at about the same time, it might be 1967. I didn't win a major that year, and, in fact, after finishing fourth in the Masters, I suffered another disappointing setback in the U.S. Open, finishing second—again!—to Jack Nicklaus at Baltusrol Golf Club in Springfield, New Jersey. On the heels of the 1966 playoff loss at Olympic Club, this was tough to take, especially when I shot 279, becoming the first man in U.S. Open history to break 280 twice. And I did it despite the first of many flare-ups of a hip injury.

But my golf was still very good that year. I successfully defended my title at the Los Angeles Open, and won three other PGA Tour titles at the Tucson Open, American Golf Classic, and Thunderbird Classic. I added the Piccadilly World Match Play Championship in England and the World Cup individual title in Mexico City. I also teamed up with

Jack to win the World Cup team title. The American Golf Classic marked my 50th win on the U.S. tour, and the $10,000 first prize that went with it gave me another milestone—the first golfer to earn more than $1 million. An interesting element in my L.A. victory, which included a second-round 64, was that I won using new aluminum shafts in my clubs. My scoring average of 70.19 for the year was good enough for my fourth Vardon Trophy as the tour's scoring leader. The only other disappointment golfing-wise was missing the Open Championship to rest my ailing right hip, which would give me more trouble in the years ahead.

But the fall was memorable as I helped the United States win another Ryder Cup, this one at Champions Golf Club in Houston. I went 5–0 for captain Ben Hogan, who decided that we would play the smaller British ball even though we were competing in the U.S. The final score was 23½ to 8½, which somewhat validated Hogan's introduction of us during the gala dinner as "the best golfers in the world." The Britons were rather sore over that remark. I nearly choked on my dinner when I heard that. The 15-point margin is still the largest in Ryder Cup history.

The most memorable victory for me came in a Saturday afternoon four-ball match with Julius Boros against Hugh Boyle and George Will of Great Britain and Ireland, who birdied four of the first seven holes for a 3-up lead. As we were walking to the eighth tee, Hogan and Jackie Burke approached. Jackie was co-owner of Champions Club with Jimmy Demaret.

Hogan said nothing, but Burke, a crusty sort, was ready

to needle Boros and me. He said with his South Texas drawl, "I've been hearing about all those . . . charges you make. I'd like to see ya make a charge out of this one."

Then he issued a challenge of sorts. "I'll tell you what I'll do; if you beat these guys, I'll build you a handmade clock."

A clock? Okay. I thought that was a bit odd, but when Julius and I made a birdie to win 1-up, I spotted Burke and Hogan standing behind the green. I said to Jack as I walked on by, "I'll be expecting my clock." A few weeks later my clock arrived with the letters A-R-N-O-L-D-P-A-L-M-E-R replacing the usual numbers on the clockface, and it still sits on a shelf in my workroom in Latrobe.

As for off the golf course, I was very busy and things got much busier. In January, *Golf Magazine* published an instructional compendium under my byline titled, "The Best Golf Tips I Know." Maybe that's why I played so well that year.

On January 9, I was one of eight inaugural selections for the governor's Committee of 100,000 Pennsylvanians, which was created to recognize people from the state or who live in the state who somehow distinguished themselves. Among the other recipients were Dr. Jonas Salk, who discovered a vaccine for polio in 1954, Thomas B. McCabe, former chairman of the Federal Reserve Board, and artist Andrew Wyeth. Whoa. Heady company. And then the following day my good friend, former President Dwight Eisenhower, sent a telegram informing me that I'd been conferred an honorary membership at Cherry Hills Country Club, site of my 1960 U.S. Open victory.

Things only got more interesting from there. On the last

day of February we opened the first Arnold Palmer Indoor Golf School, where I hit the first ceremonial tee shot. My hope was that we'd become known as "the Harvard of golf schools."

Also by 1967 we had more than 100 dry-cleaning centers across the country. How did we get into the laundry business? Sometimes I ask myself that same question, but it turned out to be another shrewd move with a push from McCormack.

Mark had received a letter from former pro tennis player Sidney Wood requesting a meeting to discuss dry-cleaning franchises. Sidney apparently could talk a good game. Mark was very skeptical at first, but Sidney apparently had it all figured out, having gotten into the business himself while his contemporaries were retiring to jobs as stock brokers or insurance agents. Sidney's theory was that if you knew your laundryman well, you would trust him with your business.

The concept of trust always was important to me. It was the basis of my agreement with Mark and with all my business deals. But I thought it was a crazy idea. My business was golf. I told Mark, "People are going to be coming up to me in the clubhouse and saying I ruined their pants." When I told some of my fellow golfers about the idea, they laughed. Dave Marr in particular thought it wasn't going to work.

But assured repeatedly by Mark that this was a potentially lucrative move, we pushed forward. We contacted George Strike, president of American Laundry Machinery Company, and started the Arnold Palmer Cleaning Centers. The centers featured a golf décor, like a golf course clubhouse, and all the employees wore grass-green sports coats. These cleaning centers, we found, were breaking even in an average of eight to ten weeks, far faster than the average competitor, who needed almost nine months to show a profit. I had become a dry-cleaning magnate on the simple concept that if two dry cleaners were in close proximity and one was called Arnold Palmer's and the other isn't, the Palmer shop has a better chance of succeeding based on name recognition and trust. This, in turn, Mark figured, meant that no field was not feasible for an Arnold Palmer franchise. Bet you didn't know this, but that meant even Christmas trees. That's right, JCPenney made a thorough study of the possibility of marketing such trees for the 1967 Christmas season.

Which reminds me of a passage from a *Wall Street Journal* story from around the same time that began: "Who can supply you with a complete golf outfit from clubs to socks, dry clean your clothes, put an ice-skating rink in your back yard, steer you to the right place to get stock certificates printed and then go out and shoot 68? Superman? Not quite. Arnold Palmer. He is a business unto himself."

The overwhelming success of the dry-cleaning franchises and these other divisions of Arnold Palmer Enterprises led to a substantial business relationship with National Broadcasting Co. The deal, which was reported in March of '67 in several newspapers, but not finalized until later, entailed NBC's acquisition of several of my businesses. In addition, I agreed to appear on-air exclusively for the network as a golf analyst and to help develop other sports programming. The arrangement, in which APE became a subsidiary of NBC (though I maintained control) seemed like a natural for several reasons, one big one being that I already had a relationship with RCA, which was NBC's parent.

My business ties with NBC have since ended, but I still enjoy a great relationship with the network through my tournament, the Arnold Palmer Invitational Presented by Master-Card. NBC and Golf Channel, which are now partners, share the broadcasting of the tournament.

There always was a belief among some of my critics that I spread myself too thin and this cost me a number of golf tournaments. I'll admit that for a time I didn't prioritize my golf and business in an effective manner. Eventually, however, I managed to strike a balance, and this was a year that proved to me that I could handle all of my responsibilities in a way that allowed me to flourish in both aspects. It took a bit more discipline, which was another quality that my father always preached.

THE ART OF TEA

———

ARNOLD PALMER TEA is 100 percent my creation—made up, roughly, of 75 percent tea and 25 percent lemonade . . . tea has to dominate or it isn't quite right—but I never called it an Arnold Palmer. In fact, I never really called it anything at all except iced tea and lemonade.

Let me set the record straight on its origin, as I did in an ESPN *30 for 30* TV feature on the subject. (No, I can't believe it was worth all that effort, either, but it was very nice all the same.) Here's the story: I concocted it one afternoon with the help of my wife, Winnie. She had made a lot of iced tea for lunch, and I said, "Hey babe, I've got an idea. You make the iced tea in a big pitcher, and we'll just put a little lemonade in it and see how that works." I had it for lunch after working on the golf course. I thought, "Boy, this is great. I'm going to take it with me when I play golf." I did that often, and I made sure that it was available at Latrobe Country Club and Bay Hill Club.

Not too many years later I was in a Palm Springs restaurant ordering a drink after a long day designing a golf course out there. I told the waitress to mix a drink for me to certain specifications—iced tea with a healthy splash of lemonade. A woman sitting nearby overhead me, and she told the waitress, "I want what he ordered. I want an Arnold Palmer." Slowly, the name caught on with the popularity of the concoction. But it didn't occur to us to try to market Arnold Palmer tea for quite some time, even though it was popular in Palm Springs and mostly the West Coast.

But our first attempt wasn't successful. Like many business ideas, there are bumps in the road before you can make it work, and in the early 1990s we tried to market and sell the iced tea as a finished product, but the licensee with which we had an agreement couldn't push it out to market effectively.

Now fast-forward to 2001, and an Orlando businessman named Chris Byrd, who lived near Bay Hill and had been a fan of mine going back to his teen years, came up with a marketing proposal that he pitched the day after that year's Arnold Palmer Invitational Presented by MasterCard (then called the Bay Hill Invitational Presented by Cooper Tires). I liked what he had to say, the ideas that he put forth, and then Chris went out and created a management company, Innovative Flavors LLC, with a plan of licensing dairies and tea manufacturers throughout the U.S. to process and package the product under strict quality assurance guidelines.

Eventually, an agreement was struck with Arizona Beverages to license and manufacture a shelf-stable version sold in a 23-ounce can. Then things really started to take off. Arizona experienced multiple years of 100 percent growth in the Arnold Palmer line of beverages and today we sell over 400 million cans annually.

I'm often asked what I think when people order an Arnold Palmer in front of me. Frankly, I'm a little embarrassed, but I'm happy they're ordering it. I like to think that maybe I've created something that is fun. And it has been fun for me. I have one or two every day. And when I order it, I just say, "I'll have a Palmer." I don't think about it in the first person. Alastair Johnston once said that the Arnold Palmer (the drink) is successful because it's not a product that I endorse. It's the actual name of the product. "It's totally authentic," Alastair has claimed.

It should be authentic because that was my approach throughout my career. It sure paid off for me—and for that other Arnold Palmer.

BAY HILL

————

SOMETIMES A BUSINESS deal that comes with its share of bad publicity is a bad deal. So it was with our near sale of Bay Hill Club & Lodge in the mid-1980s. It wasn't a deal that was going to end up severing my ties with the club; I never would let that happen no matter how much money was involved.

A group of Japanese businessmen offered an eye-popping amount of money. This, of course, was during a period when Japan's economy was booming and they were buying up golf courses, including Pebble Beach Golf Links. In the case of Bay Hill, the interested party in question was putting roughly $50 million on the table for the entire 200-plus-acre complex. This was considerably more than the money I paid for it, plus whatever I had poured into it through the years to make the golf course and the lodge top-notch in every way possible.

I first visited Orlando in 1948 with the Wake Forest golf

team to play golf against Rollins College, and I knew then that someday I would be back. I didn't know to what extent I would be here, but I liked the small-town atmosphere, the orange groves, the pristine lakes, and the surrounding areas.

My initial encounter with Bay Hill came in 1962 when I was down in Orlando to play in the Citrus Open. It was still raw then, but a few years later, on February 28, 1965, I played in an exhibition match at Bay Hill sponsored by the Orlando Jaycees against local favorite Dave Ragan, Don Cherry, quite a good singer as well as a golfer, and Jack Nicklaus. The golf course, which opened in late November 1961, was tough— no member broke 80 on opening day—but perhaps because my good buddy and rival Mr. Nicklaus was along for the ride, I played rather nicely. I birdied the first, third, and fourth holes and rode that to a 6-under-par 66. None of the other three gentlemen broke par, with Jack finishing second with a 73. Like I said, the course was difficult. But I liked it right away. As I told the media in the immediate aftermath, "It's a course that makes you hit your shots." I thought it was an excellent design by Dick Wilson, but I did see ways to improve it, and I enacted those improvements once I acquired the property.

After the exhibition, I returned to the house we were renting in Coral Gables and said to Winnie, "Babe I've just played the best golf course in Florida, and I want to own it." I suppose you could say that my feelings were somewhat similar to how I felt about Winnie when we first met. I just had a feeling. It was another love-at-first-sight kind of moment for me.

When she laid eyes on it, Winnie agreed that it was a wonderful place, secluded, plentiful orange groves and wildlife around, and in a part of Florida that was rather undeveloped and laid-back. Four years later, we finalized a five-year lease with an option to buy the club from a group of owners from Nashville and Detroit. And in 1974, through a rather complicated set of transactions, we finally and officially acquired the golf club and surrounding property. Little did we know that things were going to change quickly—and everyone thought that I was very, very intelligent to know that Disney World was going to be built just down the road from Bay Hill. Well, frankly, I think Disney World is great, and I think what has happened is fantastic. On the other hand, I didn't want that to happen. I was looking for a small golf course in a rural community that would be similar to Latrobe, and Disney ruined that. But it was great for our investment.

Speaking of Latrobe, three years before we completed the purchase of Bay Hill, Winnie and I became the sole stockholders in Latrobe Country Club. That meant Pap had to work for me, and when I chided him about this little business arrangement, he didn't find it particularly amusing. But our yearly schedule was set; we would spend winter at Bay Hill and summer and parts of spring and fall in Latrobe. It was perfect.

So there I was a little more than a decade later, owner of two golf clubs, looking at a $50 million windfall if I sold one of them. But it just wasn't that easy. And, in fact, it turned into a huge and costly headache. When the news started circulating that we might sell Bay Hill to Japanese investors, we received criticism from just about every corner. And there were sensitivity issues as well; the community in and around Bay Hill was home to a number of World War II veterans who weren't particularly accepting of the idea of a Japanese group owning Bay Hill.

But because I had business partners to consider, and because I would continue to run the day-to-day operations and remain tied to the club after handing over the keys, I had to give the offer serious consideration. But a deal too good to be true usually is, and that was the case in this instance. Perhaps because their financial situation wasn't nearly as solid as we were led to believe, the Japanese group used a loophole in the proposed agreement to back out, forfeiting a substantial nonrefundable deposit.

But even if this had not been the case, I was coming around to the realization that the deal just didn't feel right. I've had that feeling before, and most of the time my instincts were pretty good. Not perfect, mind you, but good.

DESIGN

AT MY AGE I know I am slowing down physically. Let's face it, they don't give you a pacemaker, which I received in 2014, if you're getting younger. But I don't feel like I want to slow down in my life. I still have things I want to accomplish.

One area where I still have a tremendous desire to keep going is in golf course design. A visitor in my office at Bay Hill late in 2015 wanted to know what I was working on with my design team. Of course the most heavily publicized project was the golf course near The Greenbrier in West Virginia that I was designing with my good old friends Jack Nicklaus, Gary Player, and Lee Trevino. In fact, I had just come from a meeting among the four of us a few days earlier, and it was quite an experience being with those three guys again. I did a lot of listening, that's for sure. I could hardly get a word in. But it was all fun.

The piece of ground on which we are designing the 8,000-yard golf course is one of the most challenging I have ever worked on. It is very dramatic, with strong elevation. Jim Justice, the owner of The Greenbrier, and the developer of this new layout, wants us to build a golf course that could host a U.S. Open championship. We're going to do our darndest to give him one. Considering that together we have won eight U.S. Opens, I think we know what we are doing.

It's funny how my career in golf has segued from playing to course design. My first-grade teacher told me I should be an artist when I grow up. In a way she turned out to be prophetic. I feel like an artist, just not with a canvas and paint. Over the years I have been fortunate enough to design more than 300 courses, many with the late Ed Seay, who was a tremendous architect and was a great friend who complemented me in the field.

It was around the mid-1980s when I really felt strongly about doing more as a course designer. I told a group of reporters at the time, "Imagine twenty or thirty years ago, all I wanted to do was play. Now, I just want to make the game as fascinating for others as it is for me. I'm really more interested these days in designing than playing. I've been to Japan, Thailand, Italy, Ireland, Scotland, Taiwan, and China and the business is growing like mad." And it was growing, and I can tell you that I enjoyed it immensely, and one of the reasons was I felt like I could really contribute something to the game this way. I had played golf all over the world, and so I thought I had the kind of ideas that translated well to helping other people enjoy the game. Enjoyment of the game was my bottom line, too. I wanted to build courses that were fun and that looked pretty. I tried not to design too many courses that anyone would consider difficult.

The design business isn't growing nearly as quickly now, but I'm still quite busy.

I've never told anyone this until now, but I still have a plan to build what I consider the ultimate golf course. I've thought about it for a long time. I have a few other interesting ideas I'd want to try out. Now I have to find someone who would want to build this dream course. Like I said, I still have things I want to accomplish.

DO WHAT YOU LOVE

IF YOU DON'T LIKE what you're doing in life, then you probably shouldn't be doing it. From the standpoint of what you do with your life professionally, do your job so that when you walk out at night, you're proud of what you did that day.

I've always had the advantage of loving what I was doing, and any sacrifices I had to make weren't as great as the rewards that I was receiving.

"Well, Arnie," you might say, "that's easy for you because you played golf for a living. Who wouldn't want to do that?"

Sure, I derived tremendous pleasure and financial gain from playing golf for a living. I'd do it all again in a heartbeat. But if golf hadn't worked out, I'd have found something else just as meaningful to me. It wouldn't have been selling paint, as I did after leaving the Coast Guard, the job I had when I won the U.S. Amateur in 1954. But I've written earlier about the fact that I would have probably become an airline pilot. I loved flying that much. I suppose in one respect I am very lucky that I did two things well that I truly enjoyed.

But the point is that you can always make a change in your life to do what you want. And what will drive you, what should drive you, is your pride. I've never seen anyone be successful who didn't have pride. Have pride in yourself and set goals that reflect that pride. Do that and you will succeed, whatever it is you choose to do with your professional life.

INSTINCTS

———

ONE OF MY STRONGEST PHILOSOPHIES on business is very basic: an aversion to risk. This probably sounds a little contrary to my nature because of the whole go-for-broke style of golf and the risks that I took on the golf course. But that's not to say I never took on any risks; I just always made sure to minimize risk wherever possible, and if I couldn't, then I would walk away, even if it seemed like the payoff might be attractive.

An exception was the start of Golf Channel. My advisors were against it. Strongly. But Joe Gibbs, a businessman from Birmingham, Alabama, who was the brains behind the idea, was a persuasive man. And he was prepared.

I had met Joe in 1990 when he hosted me at his home during the PGA Championship at Shoal Creek. Joe was a cable entrepreneur who already had built three successful cable and communication companies and had the experience to launch a network. But his inexperience with golf hampered him in his latest initiative, and he needed someone with knowledge of the game and the people in it to raise the necessary investment funds to get it off the ground.

I'll admit, I thought the idea of a twenty-four-hour cable network devoted to golf was a good one, but it also seemed like a stretch. The primary question I had was what we would put on the air for twenty-four hours a day. Well, Joe had the answer. He was very good with his foresight and thinking. My advisors still thought it was too risky, but I was satisfied with everything Joe was telling me. Finally, I had to make a decision. And I just said, "Gentlemen, if I hadn't tried to hit it through the tree a few times in my life, none of us would be here. Let's do this."

We announced the launch of Golf Channel at the 1993 Bob Hope Chrysler Classic, and we were able to secure some important backing, most notably six of the country's leading cable operators, which gave us a reliable avenue of distribution. With headquarters in Orlando, not far from Bay Hill Club, we launched on January 17, 1995, with the first fully digital production facility in the United States.

We had a varied programming schedule, but not a lot of live golf at the time. That changed as we grew and evolved, and today Golf Channel is available in more than 120 million homes in eighty-three countries and is broadcast in twelve languages.

One of the nicest things that happened to me with respect to Golf Channel occurred on January 29, 2013, when I cut the ribbon at Golf Channel Studios to officially christen *Morning*

Drive's new set named in my honor as "Studio AP." In addition to revealing the new state-of-the-art studio, I had a chance to introduce Golf Channel's new autograph board that is signed by every guest that visits *Morning Drive.*

"Arnold Palmer is not only Golf Channel's co-founder, but also now one of *Morning Drive*'s most loyal viewers, so we are proud to be naming *Morning Drive*'s new studio after him," Golf Channel president Mike McCarley said, offering some nice words at the time. "*Morning Drive*'s new editorial philosophy is to showcase golf as a lifestyle for a lifetime, just as Mr. Palmer has enjoyed all aspects of the game since first swinging a club at age 3."

I think if there is any lesson at all in my involvement with Golf Channel, it's simply to trust your instincts. And trust your background, too. Move forward if you're presented with an opportunity that matches up with the things in your life with which you are familiar and which line up with your overall philosophy. Yes, Golf Channel was a big risk, but it was one that I thought I could manage and that I thought had a good chance of succeeding based on things I knew about the game.

That's very important. The risk was still contained within my field of expertise and knowledge. That is an important distinction to make. I'm glad I was proven right.

A MAN'S WORD

I'VE ALREADY MENTIONED the epic handshake agreement I shared with Mark McCormack that was our bond of trust throughout our long association. My longtime design associate, the late Ed Seay, also was a wonderful partner with whom I never had a written agreement. We shook hands on collaborative design business in 1970 after working with another designer, Frank Duane, for about five years. A former U.S. Marine, Ed was the one who suggested that we not sign any type of lengthy legal document. Our word was going to be our bond. I knew I had found the perfect partner.

As I mentioned earlier, when I turned professional in late 1954, I did sign a contract with Wilson Sporting Goods, a basic staff contract that didn't have many frills beyond their paying me $5,000 annually and providing me with clubs, balls, and a Wilson staff bag with my name on the front of it. I couldn't have been happier with the deal. I liked everyone at the company and the fact that Fred Bowman, the president of the company, had shaken my hand and told me that if at any time I wanted to sever my relationship with the company, they would honor that request. I took him at his word, and after an initial three-year deal I signed a second one.

But when Mark came on board and started looking more closely at the deal, it was apparent that it wasn't quite as good as I was led to believe. For one thing, in 1960, when I thought the deal had come to its conclusion, I learned that there was a tiny clause in the contract that automatically renewed it for another three years, strictly at Wilson's option. I had just won my second Masters when I learned this. You think they didn't want to hang on to me? For another, I had no say in the quality or distribution of the equipment that went out under my name. When I tried to get involved, with all the experience I had working with clubs, I was basically told to shove off. Then there was another section that basically prevented me from earning a nickel anywhere in the world without Wilson's approval. In short, there were a lot of issues with it. Restricted from the ability to market my name and likeness as I saw fit was just the most onerous part of the equation.

We asked for a meeting with Wilson, and Bill Holmes, who had succeeded Fred Bowman as president, agreed to see us the week after the 1960 Tournament of Champions. Bill told us all about the great things Wilson was going to do on my behalf, and after about two hours, Mark piped up and asked a crucial question. "Mr. Holmes," he said, "let me ask you a question. If Arnold requested a release from his Wilson contract based on his assurances given to him by

Mr. Bowman and others some time back, would you grant him that release?"

After three or four seconds that seemed like minutes, Holmes finally said, "No, we would not."

Well, there it was. I could not have been more disappointed. Our good working relationship with Wilson ended that day, though we did try to work out several other deals that either would have allowed me to buy out my contract at considerable financial cost or come up with a more equitable deal. Nothing could be done, even though Mark worked long and hard to find some common ground.

In fact, Mark had worked with Wilson executives on an innovative set of solutions including deferred compensation and more commercial endorsement freedom. Just about all parties were in agreement, but the deal still had to be approved by Judge James Cooney, Wilson's legendary chairman. He took one look at it and tossed it aside and began to lecture Mark and me, and asked who was Arnold Palmer to try to dictate terms to him and Wilson when he already had Patty Berg and Sam Snead under contract.

I ended up riding out the string honorably until November of 1963. Then, as Mark had wanted to do anyway, I started Arnold Palmer Golf Company and never looked back. I also wasn't allowed many more handshake agreements, as per instructions from Mark. However, Ed Seay, my longtime golf course design associate, was one wonderful exception, and he renewed my faith in what I call honorable business practices.

HANDS-ON

———

ALTHOUGH I HAVE NEVER neglected my golf game, even during my busiest times—as anyone who has seen me hitting balls into a net behind my office in Latrobe or practicing at Bay Hill can attest—I have always tried to be a hands-on person in regards to all my businesses. A good, strong grip works well in business as well as golf. That doesn't mean I haven't had capable people oversee certain aspects of each enterprise; that's a necessity. But there hasn't been a significant decision made where I wasn't directly involved.

I think the source of this, again, is my father and the way he went about doing his job at Latrobe Country Club.

Sometimes my natural instincts to be on top of things might have been construed as putting business before golf. One person who thought that this might be true, ironically, was Pap.

My father didn't often speak to the press, but in the middle of a somewhat lackluster 1963 season, he spoke via telephone to the Associated Press about my many outside interests. "There's nothing wrong with Arnie's golf. He's just got too many darned irons in the fire," Pap was quoted as saying. His comments came on the heels of losing the Masters to Jack Nicklaus and then watching Jack best me again in the Tournament of Champions.

Pap's main message was that in the past I could get away with attending to my many business pursuits and still win tournaments, but not with someone now coming along as talented and as ambitious as Jack was. Now, my "lackluster" year wasn't too shabby. I won six times on the tour, another event in Australia, and added a victory in the Canada Cup, teaming with that guy Nicklaus in representing the United States.

But Pap understood that I was simply acting as I was taught—by him—and in a manner that satisfied my natural desire to succeed and be in control. It's why I learned how to fly my own plane. And growing up, Pap made sure I saw the sunrise plenty of times, and I saw how his attention to myriad details was the only way to do things properly. Plus, I have always been a restless sort who has to remain busy, so a full day was never a day I dreaded.

There were other forces at work. Growing up in the Depression, I learned the value of a dollar, and I was never very comfortable not having a good grasp of my affairs. Then there was my sense of responsibility. I couldn't in good conscience enter into any business arrangement and not give my all. If someone wanted to do business with Arnold Palmer, well, they were going to get Arnold Palmer. Finally, I'll admit that I'm a bit of a perfectionist who simply wanted a decision-making role in my enterprise. There was only one way to accomplish all that I wanted to do, and that was to be personally engaged.

But there's another tale I have to tell that illustrates perfectly why it's necessary to make sure you have your finger on the pulse of your entire enterprise. It's just smart business.

HANDS-OFF

———

I ONCE LOST $14 MILLION on a Ford Taurus. The good news is that I wasn't alone; Mark McCormack also lost $14 million on the same deal. That's oversimplifying things, but that was more or less the upshot of one of the more painful experiences for me under the Arnold Palmer Enterprises umbrella.

In 1990, Arnold Palmer Automotive Group generated revenues of $491 million, and it was ranked 388th by *Forbes* among top 400 companies in U.S. It was the first time the company had made the list.

The man who ran the company was a trusted friend named Jim O'Neal, whom I had known since 1976. Jim was a bit eccentric, to say the least. When he traveled around the U.S. on business, he would have six or more cases with him. In essence, he carried around the entire company with him in trunks. Obviously, things were going well with Jim

at the helm as he oversaw my chain of six automobile dealerships.

But our success wasn't all that it seemed. As widely reported, O'Neal had leveraged my business relationship with
Hertz, in which I was its leading spokesman, to sell automo-
biles to the rental car company through my dealerships in the
late 1980s and early 1990s. Not only did I have my Cadillac,
Pontiac, Buick, and Oldsmobile dealership in Latrobe, but
also a Cadillac dealership in Charlotte, a Chevrolet dealership
in Kentucky, a Lincoln-Mercury dealership in Hilton Head,
and a Ford dealership in California. I won't get into the full
ins and outs of the deals, but the dealerships eventually had
to buy back the cars, and in the case of the Ford Taurus, there
was a very small margin of profit in the sale to Hertz. But the
depreciation of those cars made them worth much less than
the agreed-to buyback price.

We're talking here about a lot of cars. Which is why, when
the deal unraveled, as it had to do, McCormack and I were
on the hook for a huge loss. O'Neal's overreach and unchecked
ambition made for a shockingly poor arrangement, and we
paid dearly.

At the end of it all, I learned the hard way that there are
times when you really shouldn't mix business and friendship,
and this episode was a tough reminder about keeping tabs on
things religiously. My not being hands-on in this situation,
as I had in so many other aspects of my business, was very
costly, and it saddened me in that it ended a longtime friendship. That was even more painful, and that's why it troubles
me even to this day.

LISTENING

———

My father gave me so many great pieces of advice. He wasn't an educated man, but he was intelligent and filled with simple common sense that proved so much more valuable than a formal education.

He drilled one thing into my head when it came to dealing with people in a working environment and that was the importance of being a good listener. He figured that he would just as soon let the other guy talk as much as he wants. Chances are he was going to tell you everything he knew and somewhere in there he was going to tell you everything you wanted to know about him and about the subject at hand.

I took that advice to heart more than just about anything else he taught me. Why? I didn't feel particularly intelligent about the many aspects of business that I encountered. Well, I can say it more forcefully than that; I felt stupid. But that was okay, because I was smart enough to know that the best thing I could do is keep my mouth shut and learn from those around me.

It's not an easy thing to do. We all want to participate in a meeting or a conversation and maybe show a little bit of just how much we know or how smart we are. The temptation is great. But you have to fight it. There will come a time to speak your mind. That might take a few minutes or much longer.

I remember being summoned into a meeting in California with President Nixon to discuss the Vietnam War. I was playing in Bob Hope's tournament, and Bob and I both were invited to Nixon's home in San Clemente. I had no idea at the time why he was inviting me to a presidential meeting, but I was interested to find out.

When Bob and I got off the U.S. Marine helicopter that had taken us to Nixon's residence, we found Secretary of State Henry Kissinger, Vice President Gerald Ford, and other members of the president's national security team gathered in the living room. It soon was impressed upon me that the president wanted my thoughts—a working-class kid from Pennsylvania—on how best to end the conflict over there. Like many Americans, I was becoming more distraught over the fighting in Southeast Asia and wondered what our objective was supposed to be.

I knew enough about the war to have an opinion. I always paid attention to world events. But when we sat down with the president, the last thing I was going to do was speak my mind as the group discussed various strategic options and their respective consequences.

My thought was that we should get the fighting over as

soon as possible. When the president looked in my direction and asked what I thought, I was still reluctant to offer an opinion. But everyone was looking at me. Finally, I said we should "go for the green" and end the war quickly. Everyone laughed at my golf analogy, but I wasn't really trying to be funny. That was my opinion.

I sure learned a heck of a lot about geopolitics that day, among other things. But you can only learn from listening, and I have applied that rule of thumb to situations big and small.

Usually, the rewards were just big.

PEBBLE BEACH

————

YOU CAN PROBABLY GUESS the golf courses that are near and dear to my heart. Bay Hill Club & Lodge and Latrobe Country Club are obviously at the top of my list, with Augusta National Golf Club following very close behind. I've already mentioned Pine Valley and The Greenbrier as places that hold some significance to me personally. Cherry Hills Country Club, where I won my U.S. Open, is very special. I didn't win at St. Andrews, but that is where my long relationship with the Open Championship and the good folks of the R&A began, and receiving my honorary degree from the University of St. Andrews in 2011 adds to that deep affection.

You can put Pebble Beach Golf Links into the same category as St. Andrews—another gorgeous seaside golf course for which I hold great affection despite never having won a tournament there. Of course, the fact that I am one of the principal owners of Pebble Beach has something to do with this, but my appreciation for Pebble Beach long preceded my decision to invest in the iconic layout that remains a daily fee golf course, and, thus, is available to the public golfer. That makes it quite special.

The whole area of Pebble Beach is conducive to good golf and enjoying golf. That's what draws golfers there and the nongolfers who just want to experience a true natural wonder. It's safe to say that Pebble Beach Golf Links is on every golfer's bucket list.

I always considered it special, though it was an unrequited love. I competed in the Bing Crosby Clambake—now the AT&T Pebble Beach Pro-Am—for more than twenty years starting in 1958, and although I played well in it and had a few great chances to win, I never quite got over the hump. I also had a chance to win the 1972 U.S. Open at Pebble Beach, but an opening 77 and a closing 76 did me in, and I finished third while Jack Nicklaus went on to victory. But to illustrate just how painfully close I was to winning, there was a particular juncture in the final round that appeared on split-screen on television. I was putting for birdie on 14 and Jack had a par putt on No. 12. If I made mine and Jack missed, I'd have taken the lead. The opposite occurred, however, and I had to settle for merely another good finish in the Open.

But if there was one incident in particular that stands out for me at Pebble Beach above all others, it's what happened in the 1967 Crosby. I came to the par-5 14th hole trailing Nicklaus by a stroke, and I was in my usual aggressive mindset, going for the green in two shots. Instead, however, I pushed my approach to the right, and the ball hit a tree and caromed out of bounds. I dropped and tried again and hit the same tree with that shot, and it went out of bounds again. Eventually, I took a nine on the hole and finished third behind Jack and Bill Casper.

A storm blew through the course that night and uprooted the tree. Some say nature tried to make it up to me. I say too late.

The group that completed the deal for Pebble Beach in 1999—after it had changed hands a couple of times already in the previous ten years—included actor Clint Eastwood, former baseball commissioner Peter Ueberroth, and airline executive Dick Ferris. The purchase also included Spyglass Hill Golf Course, The Links at Spanish Bay, and Del Monte Golf Course, plus the Lodge at Pebble Beach, the Inn at Spanish Bay, and 17-Mile Drive, which winds through Pebble Beach and nearby Del Monte Forest. I derive great enjoyment from the partnership with people I consider great friends, and it's turned out to be a good deal. In fact, I consider it one of the greatest business decisions I've ever made. It's more about the prestige of association with Pebble Beach than any capital concerns, though we still make a little money on it.

We all have our jobs when it comes to the property. Mine is making sure the golf course is up to date and up to snuff. We've already begun making preparations for the 2019 U.S. Open, which will be held during Pebble's centennial year. A major renovation of the 17th hole already is receiving many compliments. We've done a few things with the 14th green, and we've undertaken a few other tweaks here and there. To clarify: we didn't change things so much as we updated them, like giving the sand traps a more modern look and in some cases relocating them to have an impact on how the top professional golfers play the game.

I've told some people that my involvement in the acquisition of Pebble Beach was purely a business opportunity with the right people. It was a project that we had been looking at and studying for many years, so when the time was right, we were ready. The decision was a no-brainer as far as I was concerned. But there was much more to it than just business. Pebble Beach hasn't been a special place just for me. The place is full of history and tradition. We wanted to preserve these traditions and continue to enhance one of the finest golf experiences in the world.

You know, it was probably going for broke a little bit, I must say, but it was something that I felt would be a very good thing, and it has worked out wonderfully.

QUALITY

I FIRST DROVE A CADILLAC while I was still attending college at Wake Forest. My best friend Bud Worsham and I had gone to Latrobe to visit my parents for the weekend. We did this often, either going to Latrobe or to his folks' home in Maryland.

One pleasant Sunday afternoon while we were hitchhiking back to Winston-Salem, we accepted a ride south of Washington on U.S. Route 1 from a gentleman who just so happened to be a golfer. This was obviously in the day when you didn't worry about hitching a ride, and neither did good folks worry about picking up two college-aged kids. Of course, we were carrying our golf clubs, so we didn't exactly look too threatening.

Seeing our clubs probably was the reason this kind gentleman stopped. He happened to be tour golfer George Fazio, who later in his career went on to become a respected golf course architect while teaming with his nephew Tom. I recognized him instantly. And he knew Bud's older brother, Lew. So we formed an instant bond.

He asked Bud and me if one of us was old enough to drive, and I quickly piped up. Fazio eased into the backseat and took a nap, asking us to wake him when we reached North Carolina while I got behind the wheel and Bud got in the passenger seat. I'll never forget the smooth ride of that car and the way it looked and felt with its refined interior—a true symbol of American success.

I have been an avid fan of the Cadillac brand ever since, and I still drive one to this day, a nice, big SUV model that sort of fits my personality and image as a driver. I get a new one every season from the Cadillac dealer around the corner a few miles from my house in Latrobe. I trust that dealer—and I had better. It's called Arnold Palmer Motors!

I feel about a Cadillac the same way I feel about Rolex, with whom I've had a fifty-year relationship. It isn't about being showy or about owning something expensive. Certainly growing up not having a lot of money, owning something like a Rolex watch was a dream. And it was a dream I never thought I'd realize. It was about aspiring to success, which a brand like Cadillac or Rolex symbolized. It was about living the American Dream, if you will, something all of us hope to realize. So I am grateful for the association with such a fine company like Rolex, a partnership that actually started in Japan when I became friends with André Heiniger, who was the second CEO of Rolex after the founder Hans Wilsdorf.

I also felt like there was a psychological benefit to these

associations. Being around successful people or being associated with successful enterprises puts you in a proper frame of mind about the things you want to do with your life and career. Their attitude tends to rub off on you. Winning does breed winning, on and off the course—and in my mind I think they tend to have a reciprocal application.

I don't mean to make this sound like a marketing pitch right here. It's about quality and the image I wanted to project, which also was about being the best. That was important to my own brand, to use a marketing term. Being an ambassador for Rolex or a spokesman or having a long-standing relationship with the likes of MasterCard, as I do today, are part of my overall business philosophy of joining forces with quality names and products. But I felt the same way about Pennzoil and Hertz and so many other companies with which I had a business relationship. If the company made a good product, and I genuinely liked what they were doing, then that was good enough for me.

I think that approach has been a great thing for me. And it's worked for my partners, too.

NO MEANS . . .

———

THE ABILITY TO LEARN how to say no forcefully or graciously or with conviction is an indispensable attribute for someone as busy as I have been through the years. Many of the best business decisions came from respectfully declining. Some of my worst, too. But the bottom line is that I am terrible at letting the words pass my lips.

Even when Mark McCormack took over this unpleasant chore on some occasions, it didn't really insulate me from the responsibility, since, ultimately, I was the one who had to make up his mind on whether or not I was going to do something.

My aversion to the word "no" sometimes gave McCormack fits. He joked that, "In twenty-seven languages Arnold Palmer couldn't say no."

A favorite story of his entails my handling of a request from Bob Hope to appear in his movie *Call Me Bwana*. The executive producer of the movie, Harry Saltzman, had called

Mark asking if I would do the movie. At the same time, Hope was calling me asking me to do it. I sort of agreed, but then I realized all that would be involved in what was really a cameo appearance. It was going to be shot in Kenya, for starters, and there were other complications that didn't make me too eager to do it.

Mark and I looked at the schedule, and it appeared it was going to be very difficult for me to get it done. When Saltzman called again, Mark gave him the bad news: the schedule wouldn't allow a film appearance. But then Hope calls me again, and says, "Come on, Arnie, we really need you and it will be great fun." Well, how can I say no to Bob Hope?

Another round of phone calls produced the same results. Mark said no to Saltzman, but I hemmed and hawed and stammered when Hope called me yet again. Instead of saying no, I told Mark to adjust my schedule. But that took a lot of saying no to other people to get the schedule straightened out. Mark could only throw up his hands and laugh when it was all said and done, but it worked out because we shot the scene in England instead, and it didn't take nearly as long as we thought it might. The film was released in 1963.

It did not necessarily earn rave reviews. *The New York Times* was rather harsh in its July 4 critique of the film. The first sentence of the review, written by A. H. Weiler, began, "Bob Hope, one of the world's most celebrated traveling men, undoubtedly took the wrong turn when he hit the trail toward Africa for 'Call Me Bwana.'"

Luckily, he was a bit kinder to yours truly. Sort of. Weiler wrote, "Arnold Palmer, portraying himself with surprising ease, turns up for no reason at all, of course, to play a few screwball shots with Mr. Hope to prove that they both know what to do with a golf club even under these improbable circumstances."

Nice to know I was good at being myself.

Throughout my career I had these back-and-forth struggles within myself about when to say no to people. Or if I should say no. And how to say no. While it's easier to say no from the standpoint of simplifying your life—saying no means you don't have to do anything further—I never liked the idea of disappointing people, especially when it came to things like charity golf events and other meaningful endeavors. I was most guilty when my peers called to ask if I could play in their fund-raising golf events. This was especially tough when I had my own events and requested the presence of my golfing friends.

But I have said no plenty of times in my life. I had to just to keep my sanity and have time to eat and sleep, not to mention spend time with my family and keep my golf game in relatively good shape. As I have gotten older and slowed down, I've had to invoke the use of the word even more frequently, but I still do so only after going through a painful exercise of weighing the pros and cons of any request or proposition or call for help that crosses my desk. I can tell you this much is true: I have seldom liked it.

THE TRACTOR

———

THANKS TO MARK MCCORMACK I already was a fairly successful corporate pitchman by the time I signed on as a spokesman for Pennzoil. Founded in western Pennsylvania, Pennzoil seemed like a natural business association for a native son of the same region. I don't know why it took so long to have a business relationship with such a recognizable company that hailed from the same neck of the woods as yours truly. Especially when my father used Pennzoil in the equipment at Latrobe Country Club and I had even stayed with the regional vice president of Pennzoil, Ed Douglas, and his wife, Rita, in San Francisco when the U.S. Open was played at Olympic Club in 1955.

I thought I understood a fair amount about advertising and television promotion, but I learned a few new things when Alastair Johnston, who was looking over my affairs on behalf of IMG, and I met with Pennzoil representatives about finalizing a sponsorship deal. During the meeting I mentioned how Pap used Pennzoil, and almost as an aside I told the folks at Pennzoil how well the 1947 Toro tractor my father used at the club was still running.

Suddenly, the eyes of the Pennzoil people lit up and they were clearly excited by this bit of news, which I didn't think was very significant in the overall scheme of what we'd been talking about. But they started peppering me with more questions about this tractor. What did it look like? Where did Pap keep it?

Now, I didn't say as much, but deep down I harbored a sort of love-hate relationship with tractors. Let me explain.

Those machines had a very definite impact on the type of person I became growing up, because having to work on them taught me to be humble and to know where I came from. I think about my father and the things that he told me when I was driving a tractor. There was one type that I had to drive, a 1922 Fordson with steel wheels and spikes on it. If you didn't keep those wheels flat on the ground, and caught the edge of a hill or had too much weight on the back, the wheels would spin and tear up the golf course. And that got my attention, because the old man was about to kick my rear end all the way around that golf course if I didn't learn how to drive that tractor properly. It was like playing golf: he expected me to do what he told me to do, and I did it. Pap drove the old Toro tractor around the course every day. I think it was almost a source of comfort for club members to see him on it because that meant Deacon Palmer was watching over things.

I worked with both those tractors, and I didn't much care

for them only because they kept me from what I'd rather be doing, which was hitting balls or putting or playing a few holes. But because they didn't have power steering, they really helped me build my upper body strength when I was younger. That came in handy down the road.

Anyway, I could only laugh when one of the Pennzoil reps asked if I thought it could be used in a commercial. I said, "You better have a look at it first." I knew it still ran, but it was old, and it was a bit beat up after Pap used it for hauling sod and dragging gang mowers and aerating fairways for nearly thirty years. I had a hard time believing that this idea had much merit, that there really was a use for this old tractor.

But there was, and we shot the first commercial using the tractor in the summer of 1979, and it aired for almost a year. Before I knew it, people were asking about the tractor at almost every stop I made on tour. In the 1983 L.A. Open I played with a young rookie named Payne Stewart, and he just marveled at the number of people who were shouting to me about how they used Pennzoil and they loved that tractor. It was really something, and the ad campaign was so successful that Pennzoil started carting the tractor around to trade shows, and execs even parked it in the lobby of Pennzoil's corporate headquarters.

It was a hit. Artists have painted pictures of it, and it's been photographed more times than I can count. More than 25,000 miniature replicas of it have been sold since Dick Westman, an advertising agency executive for Pennzoil, got the bright idea to license plastic models. In 2005 PGA Tour commissioner Tim Finchem presented me with a custom-made tractor similar to Pap's model.

One afternoon I was sitting in the dining room at the Beverly Hills Hotel when Bob Hope approached my table and said, "Hey, I knew you were here. I saw your tractor double-parked out front." Johnny Carson once joked on his show that I had such devoted fans that they probably could be seen walking around the golf course with quarts of Pennzoil in their pockets.

Over the years the tractor has come to be known as Arnie's Tractor—which is how Pennzoil marketed the miniature version—so my affection for the old girl changed quite a bit. It will always be Pap's tractor to me, though.

If there was a moment when I really warmed up to the thing, it was probably in 1986. I was asked to serve as grand marshal for the Latrobe Fourth of July parade, and I really made an impression when I made my entrance by flying my Hughes helicopter over the parade route before landing at Latrobe's Legion-Keener ball fields. From there I joined the parade, and the hometown folks greeted me enthusiastically— probably because I was driving a certain well-known tractor.

No matter how long you have been doing something, you can always learn something new. I sure did when it came to advertising and a beat-up old tractor, and I have to think Pap would have enjoyed watching that whole spectacle unfold with a combination of pride and bewilderment.

SENIOR MOMENTS

FOLKS WANT TO CREDIT ME with getting the Champions Tour on firm ground, and while that's a nice sentiment, I don't feel that it's accurate.

It took more people than me to make what at the start was known as the Senior PGA Tour successful. Lee Trevino, Jack Nicklaus, Gary Player, Raymond Floyd, Hale Irwin, Tom Watson, and all the other players who have come after needed to buy into the idea of senior golf and support it. Their picking up the baton was as crucial as my involvement after Sam Snead, Gardner Dickinson, Peter Thomson, and others blazed the trail with the highly successful Legends of Golf in 1978.

And I have to be honest, too; whatever I did on behalf of the senior tour was partly selfish, because I enjoyed playing golf too much when I turned fifty. It wasn't like it was something I didn't want to do or something I felt I had to do. I wanted to play senior golf, and to still try to win championships. I can tell you that winning the U.S. Senior Open in 1981 at Oakland Hills Country Club—near Detroit, a town with which I'll always feel strong emotional ties—felt every bit as good as winning the U.S. Open in 1960. Winning never gets old, as they say.

In 1980, when the Senior PGA Tour was birthed with four events, I won the PGA Seniors' Championship at Turnberry Isle Country Club in North Miami Beach, Florida, and that's a tournament that has been around since 1937 when Jock Hutchinson won it at Augusta National Golf Club. (Augusta, in fact, hosted the first two editions of the Senior PGA.) By 1983 we had sixteen tournaments, and senior golf had a solid foothold in the sports landscape.

Aside from the enjoyment I got out of continuing my competitive golf career, there was a clear business purpose for playing senior golf. It was far secondary to the lure of tournament golf, but it made good business sense to still put myself out there, to be on television in what was my long-established environment. I believe it allowed me to remain a viable corporate spokesman, and it sure didn't hurt my design business either.

The Champions Tour has been a tremendous success, and to a lesser degree than the regular tour, some players out there need to remember how things developed. The seniors, too, need to try harder to keep what they have. Did I put time into promoting senior golf? You bet I did. It was worth every minute of it, because I enjoyed myself immensely and found it rewarding to keep trying to play golf at a high level.

A LIFE'S WORK

I HAVE TO BE BUSY. It would never do for me to stop working. I will work until the very end. I don't believe that you ever stop thinking and striving to make something of your day. It's what I love. What is that law of physics about a body in motion staying in motion? Boy, that's me.

I don't keep up with everything that I used to. I'm not unaware of the fact that I have slowed down. But I have good people around me, which has always been essential in my business life. Early on it was Winnie. Then Mark Mc-Cormack. Doc Giffin has been not only a great executive assistant, but also a trusted friend for fifty years. These days I lean on Alastair Johnston and Cori Britt and a lot of other wonderful people. I also have my daughter Amy and her husband, Roy Saunders, but in the end, it is still up to me. I have to make the important decisions. And I still very much enjoy going through the process of doing that.

From a very early age watching my father I learned the value of a good day's work. It wasn't all about earning a living either. There is something satisfying about accomplishing, something in a day, building toward something, creating something, or just putting your mind through some exercises of improving on a project or task. I still get that satisfaction.

I remember drawing the ire of Joe Torre's wife in 2004 when I talked Joe, then the New York Yankees manager, out of retiring, and he signed a new contract that year with the team. I was in Maui for the Champion Skins Game and Joe and I happened to be on the same whale-watching expedition when I invited him to play golf with me at Bay Hill. Joe said, "After this year, I may be able to take you up on that." I was a bit startled by the meaning of that comment so I asked him what he was talking about. He said, "This is the last year of my contract and I'm going to be sixty-four." I just gave him a look and told him that age has nothing to do with his thinking that he should retire. I was seventy-four at the time and I told him that I was never going to retire. Joe signed a two-year contract extension for $13 million. I didn't get a commission.

Oh, I've often thought about just riding off into the sunset. But my thinking has always been that if I stop being active I wouldn't last very long. I think that would be the end of me. I can honestly say that my work ethic has been one key to living a long and happy life.

THE FINAL LESSON

I WANT TO LEAVE YOU with this thought, a confession, if you will: I never cared for the nickname "the King." At times, it has made me uncomfortable and even a bit irritated to be referred to that way. I know it was meant to be flattering, but there is no king of golf. There never has been, and there never will be.

Golf is the most democratic game on earth, a pastime of the people that grants no special privileges and pays no mind to whether a man is a hotel doorman or a corporate CEO. It punishes and exalts us all with splendid but uncompromising equal opportunity.

I'm the son of a hard-nosed golf course caretaker who had large hands and an even larger heart. He was intelligent, and he was thoughtful, but most of all, he was a man who knew the importance of priorities and respect for people and the game. He drilled into me the importance of always leaving the golf course better than I found it. I feel we have to be more vigilant than ever to make certain the things that make golf such a great game remain the same and are protected and nurtured and preserved for the next folks coming along.

I do like being called an ambassador of the game. It is a role I take very seriously, whether in my work with the USGA or with my own tournament or building a golf course or supporting the game in whatever capacity I choose to take on whenever I am in the public eye. And I hope I have set an example for everyone who loves the game to be an ambassador of sorts, too. Because we all have a responsibility to make sure this great game remains great.

Furthermore, I've always tried to be a role model, to set a good example, and sometimes I've wondered if I did a good enough job in that regard.

Mostly, however, I've simply wanted to be a golfer. And an incident that happened to me in 1991 at my own tournament at Bay Hill, then called the Nestle Invitational, reaffirmed that I was still thought of as a golfer by my fellow PGA Tour competitors. I had made the cut that year at the age of sixty-one, and unbeknownst to me, Peter Jacobsen, a good friend, decided that he was going to buy me a cake to commemorate the feat, though making the cut wasn't something I considered a feat. Peter went to a local Winn-Dixie and asked for a sheet cake for about 200 people, he told the manager, and he convinced the fellow to bake the cake that night so they could present it to me sometime that weekend.

I can't tell you how thrilled I was when the guys put that cake in front of me. As luck would have it—if you can call it that—we had a rain delay on Saturday of the tournament and just about every player who made the cut was in the locker room. Ray Floyd, Greg Norman, Jeff Sluman, Paul Azinger, Rocco Mediate, and Tom Kite were among the players who gathered around. It was a wonderful surprise. And not a bad cake, I might add.

I cut a piece for every player who was there. It was a fun afternoon, to say the least, and quite meaningful to me not just because Peter and the others went to the trouble to do that, but because I thought it said something. In my mind, it said that the guys still thought of me as one of them, that I still had a place in their world, and that they cared about what I thought and what I said.

I never wanted to be on any kind of pedestal; I never thought of myself that way, and this was an occasion when I was just one of the guys.

I have been asked about what my legacy might be, and, honestly, I've never really given it much thought. I can't put into words what the game has meant to me. And I can't tell you how great people have been to me over the years. So, if I enhanced the game and people's enjoyment of the game, I would feel like I have accomplished something.

I suppose, in the final accounting of it all, what I really am, inescapably—and how I prefer to be thought of in terms of my legacy—is a caretaker of the game, just the way my father was before me. Someone who tried to preserve it, nurture it, and improve it if he could, and who tried, also, to be a caretaker of the dignity of the game.

I hope you think I did a good job. I hope Pap thinks so, too.

ACKNOWLEDGMENTS

———

Though I have written a number of books in the past, this one was particularly important to me, because, as I delved into the process, I realized just how much I still wanted to say to my friends in golf and to fans of the game in general. Going through the exercise of getting it all down has been personally satisfying, but I couldn't have done it without a dedicated group of individuals who truly believed in this project.

I'll start with my team in Latrobe and Orlando, particularly Doc Giffin and Cori Britt, who always have been incredibly reliable and have my back. The same goes for Alastair Johnston, my longtime business advisor, who has great vision for many things, and the same was certainly true for this book.

My wife, Kit, was very supportive throughout and really understood what I was trying to accomplish. And, of course, thanks to the rest of my wonderful family, all who have contributed to my successes through the years.

A special thanks to Dave Shedloski for rolling up his sleeves and bringing great care and energy to our collaborative effort. And to Marc Resnick, Steve Cohen, and everyone at Macmillan/St. Martin's Press for guiding it along and getting us to the finish line.

And, finally, thanks to all the generations of Arnie's Army for always marching along with me on a wonderful journey.

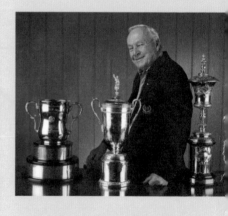